福建的世界遗产

World Heritage Sites in Fujian

福建省文化和旅游厅 策划
资源开发处 组织编写

编著
余亿明

翻译
[新西兰] Donna Jiang
[新西兰] Rocky Jiang
陈钰茜

摄影
胡家新
冯木波
王福平
赖永生
张耀辉 等

福建土楼
Fujian Tulou

海峡出版发行集团
THE STRAITS PUBLISHING & DISTRIBUTING GROUP

福建人民出版社
FUJIAN PEOPLE'S PUBLISHING HOUSE

图书在版编目（CIP）数据

福建土楼：汉英对照 / 余亿明编著；（新西兰）蒋梓青（Donna Jiang）
等译 . --福州：福建人民出版社，2020.5（2023.10重印）
（福建的世界遗产）
ISBN 978-7-211-08313-8

Ⅰ.①福… Ⅱ.①余… ②蒋… Ⅲ.①民居—古建筑
—介绍—福建—汉、英 Ⅳ.①K928.71

中国版本图书馆 CIP 数据核字（2019）第 288380 号

福建土楼
FUJIAN TULOU

作　　者：余亿明	
翻　　译：［新西兰］Donna Jiang　　［新西兰］Rocky Jiang　　陈钰茜	
责任编辑：孙　颖	
美术编辑：陈培亮	
装帧设计：［澳大利亚］Harry Wang	
内文排版：良之文化传媒	
出版发行：福建人民出版社	电　　话：0591-87533169（发行部）
网　　址：http://www.fjpph.com	电子邮箱：fjpph7211@126.com
地　　址：福州市东水路 76 号	邮政编码：350001
经　　销：福建新华发行（集团）有限责任公司	
印　　刷：雅昌文化（集团）有限公司	
地　　址：深圳市南山区深云路 19 号	
电　　话：86-755-83366138	
开　　本：787 毫米×1092 毫米　　1/16	
印　　张：18	
字　　数：404 千字	
版　　次：2020 年 5 月第 1 版	
印　　次：2023 年 10 月第 2 次印刷	
书　　号：ISBN 978-7-211-08313-8	
定　　价：108.00 元	

目 录

Contents

01

世遗档案

UNESCO's Introduction to Fujian Tulou

◎ 永定南江村土楼群。（冯木波 摄）
Nanjiang Tulou Cluster in Yongding.
(Photo by Feng Mubo)

名　　称：福建土楼
列入时间：2008年7月被正式列入《世界遗产名录》
遗产类型：世界文化遗产

　　列入《世界遗产名录》的福建土楼包括建于15世纪至20世纪的46栋建筑物，位于福建省西南部，主要分布于龙岩市永定区和漳州市南靖县、华安县。土楼是坐落在稻田、茶山和烟草地间的土制房子，大多有几层楼高，沿着一个向内、呈圆形或方形的楼层平面建造，每座建筑可容纳多达800人居住。这些建筑是为了防卫而建造，环绕着一个中央露天庭院，只有一个入口，一楼以上才有窗户，可观外面的世界。

　　一座土楼往往就是一个家族的聚居地，是村里的构成单位，被称为"家庭小王国"或"繁华的小城市"。土楼以高大的泥墙为特色，墙面由瓦屋顶覆盖，宽屋檐悬挑。最精巧的土楼建筑可追溯到17和18世纪。建筑物里，不同家庭采用垂直划分区域而居住，平均使用每个楼层，每层有两个或三个房间供每个家庭使用。与它们朴素的外表相比，土楼内部的设计则表现得相当舒适，而且常常装饰精美。

　　土楼被作为建筑传统和功能的独特代表列为世界遗产，它们体现了特殊的社区生活和防御性功能，与环境和谐共存，是人类住所的杰出范例。

◎ 南靖甘芳村大坪楼。（朱庆福 摄）
Dapinglou at Ganfang Village in Nanjing.
(Photo by Zhu Qingfu)

Fujian Tulou

Inscribed in 2008 on the World Heritage List

Cultural Property

Fujian Tulou is a property of 46 buildings constructed between the 15th and 20th centuries in the southwest of Fujian Province, mainly located in Yongding District of Longyan, and Nanjing County and Hua'an County in Zhangzhou. Set amongst rice, tea and tobacco fields, the Tulou are earthen houses. Several storeys high, they are built along an inward-looking, circular or square floor plane as housing for up to 800 people each. They were built for defence purposes around a central open courtyard with only one entrance and windows to the outside only above the first floor. Housing a whole clan, the houses functioned as village units and were known as "a little kingdom for the family" or "bustling small city". They feature tall fortified mud walls capped by tiled roofs with wide over-hanging eaves. The most elaborate structures date back to the 17th and 18th centuries. The buildings were divided vertically between families with each disposing of two or three rooms on each floor. In contrast with their plain exterior, the inside of the Tulou were built for comfort and were often highly decorated. They are inscribed as exceptional examples of a building tradition and function exemplifying a particular type of communal living and defensive organization, and, in terms of their harmonious relationship with their environment, an outstanding example of human settlement.

遗产价值

　　福建土楼是中国东南山区土楼中最具代表性、保存最完好的建筑。土楼规模宏大、建筑技艺复杂、富有戏剧性的土制防御功能，多建于13世纪至20世纪之间，巧妙地隐匿于肥沃的山谷，成为跨越时空的社群居住的杰出典范。土楼及其相关文献档案反映了700多年来，土楼这一杰出生土建筑艺术的产生、演变和发展。精心设计、分区合理的内部及精美的装饰，满足了族群的物质和精神生活需求，并以非凡的方式反映了一个地处偏远和潜在敌意的环境中发展起来的复杂小社会。大型建筑群与山水相互辉映，体现了"风水"的原则和美观、和谐的理念。

◆　土楼承载着一个特殊的见证，见证了以社区生活为目的的防御性建筑中流传下来的悠久文化，反映了复杂的建筑传统，和谐、合作的理念。尽管时间推移，记载却从未间断。

◆　土楼在规模、建筑传统和功能方面都是独一无二的，反映了广大地区在不同历史阶段的经济与社会。

◆　土楼整体，就其形式而言，是社区生活和防御需求的独特反映；就其与环境的和谐关系而言，则是人类聚居的杰出范例。

◆　保留原汁原味的土楼，关系到土楼自身及其建筑传统的延续，以及与青山、绿水及田园风光间相得益彰的关系。土楼作为一个整体，不仅在于它作为建筑物的完整性，还在于与其周围田园山林的和谐整体性。

◎ 梯田环绕的土楼人家。（王福平 摄）
A Tulou family between terraces. (Photo by Wang Fuping)

Outstanding Universal Value

Fujian Tulou are the most representative and best preserved examples of the Tulou of the mountainous regions of southeastern China. The large, technically sophisticated and dramatic earthen defensive buildings, built between the 13th and 20th centuries, in their highly sensitive setting in fertile mountain valleys, are an extraordinary reflection of a communal response to the settlement which has persisted over time. The Tulou, and their extensive associated documentary archives, reflect the emergence, innovation, and development of an outstanding art of earthen building over seven centuries. The elaborate compartmentalised interiors, some with highly decorated surfaces, met both their communities' physical and spiritual needs and reflect in an extraordinary way the development of a sophisticated society in a remote and potentially hostile environment. The relationship of the massive buildings to their landscape embodies both Feng Shui principles and ideas of landscape beauty and harmony.

◆ The Tulou bear an exceptional testimony to a long-standing cultural tradition of defensive buildings for communal living that reflect sophisticated building traditions and ideas of harmony and collaboration, well documented over time.

◆ The Tulou are exceptional in terms of size, building traditions and function, and reflect society's response to various stages in economic and social history within the wider region.

◆ The Tulou as a whole, in terms of their form are a unique reflection of communal living and defensive needs, and in terms of their harmonious relationship with their environment, an outstanding example of human settlement.

◆ The authenticity of the Tulou is related to sustaining the Tulou themselves and their building traditions as well as the structures and processes associated with their farmed and forested landscape setting. The integrity of the Tulou is related to their intactness as buildings but also to the intactness of the surrounding farmed and forested landscape.

◎ 永定洪坑村的"土楼王子"振成楼。（王福平 摄）

Zhenchenglou, the "Prince of Tulou" in Hongkeng Village of Yongding. (By Wang Fuping)

**United Nations
Educational, Scientific and
Cultural Organization** · **World Heritage
Convention**

CONVENTION CONCERNING
THE PROTECTION OF
THE WORLD CULTURAL
AND NATURAL HERITAGE

*The World Heritage Committee
has inscribed*

Fujian Tulou

on the World Heritage List

*Inscription on this List confirms the outstanding
universal value of a cultural or
natural property which requires protection for
the benefit of all humanity*

DATE OF INSCRIPTION

10 July 2008

DIRECTOR-GENERAL
OF UNESCO

O2

走近土楼

Tours around Fujian Tulou

© 方圆土楼映朝阳。（王福平 摄）
The square and circular Tulou at sunrise. (Photo by Wang Fuping)

土楼回眸——千年积淀的世界遗产

福建的土楼建造历史源远流长，最早发源于公元11世纪至13世纪的宋元时期，经过明代的发展，至清代、民国达到成熟时期。

1,000多年前，建造福建土楼的先民们几经迁徙先后来到了闽西南崇山峻岭之中，他们饱受战乱饥荒、漂泊流离之苦，选择闽粤赣交界的山区作为安身立命之所，一边要防御时常出没的虎狼野兽、盗贼匪寇的侵扰，一边要化解与土著居民的摩擦，因此，聚族而居、集体防卫成为他们赖以生存的必然选择。于是，他们传承了古老的生土建筑技艺，利用当地的生土、木材等材料，建起了福建土楼的雏形。尔后，随着建筑技艺日臻成熟，福建土楼由粗放而精细，功能也日趋完善，并经历了从方至圆再到方圆并存及各种变异形状并存的发展过程。

明成化十四年（1478），永定建县，这不仅推动了永定经济、文化的发展，也为福建土楼的发展创造了有利条件，福建土楼进入发展阶段。

◎ 南靖土楼人家。（朱庆福 摄）
A Tulou family in Nanjing. (Photo by Zhu Qingfu)

◎ 建于北宋晚期的客家人聚居村落——永定龙安寨遗址。（赖永生 供图）
The relics of Hakka Long' anzhai built in the Northern Song Dynasty. (Courtesy of Lai Yongsheng)

A World Heritage: The Past and Present of Fujian Tulou

Fujian Tulou boast a long history. The construction of the buildings began towards the end of China's Song Dynasty (between the 11th and 13th century) and continued to make developments during the Ming Dynasty. However, it was between the Qing Dynasty and the Republic of China era that the building technique truly became popular.

The ancestors of the Hakka people migrated throughout the last thousand years to the mountainous regions of Minxi (western Fujian Province). As a smaller minority group, the tight-knit Hakka people needed protection from marauding bandits and other dangers in the new territory. For both the safety and the opportunity to grow as a community, they designed a style of house that could accommodate the entire communities. With security in mind, the Hakka began with earth and wood, creating rudimentary Tulou. They then moved onto the interiors of their new, tiny village. Then, over time, the architectural techniques matured, allowing the construction and functions of the Tulou to become more extensive and refined. The shapes of the Tulou were no longer restricted to just squares and circles.

In 1478, the establishment of Yongding County gave impetus to the development of the local economy and culture, which created favourable conditions for the growth of Fujian Tulou.

到了17、18世纪的清康熙、乾隆年间，福建西南地区条丝烟、茶叶等加工业蓬勃兴起，产品销往全国及东南亚各国，当地经济发展，民众生活水平提高，对改善住宅的要求更加迫切。同时家族人口繁衍，为维护家族的共同利益，让数十数百的宗亲聚族而居，以适应家族的兴旺，势必建造更大规模的楼房，方形、圆形等土楼便应运而生，且大多规模宏大、类型多样、工艺精湛、装饰华丽，有的还融入了外来文化。福建土楼进入鼎盛阶段。

20世纪50年代以后，当地居民建造土楼更加注重实用性，结构和装饰趋于简化。这种风格一直延续至今。

长期以来，福建土楼"养在深闺人未识"，直至20世纪50年代中期，才开始得到国内现代建筑科学界的关注和赏识。由于学者的推介，20世纪60年代初，土楼研究扩及日本、美国学术界。1978年以后，随着改革开放的深入，福建土楼研究欣欣向荣。1982年以后，福建土楼引起法国、秘鲁、比利时、日本等国和中国香港、台湾等地的专家学者慕名纷纷前往实地考察，土楼研究的热潮此起彼伏，方兴未艾。

◎ 残墙断壁难掩昔日辉煌。（王福平 摄）
Ruined walls showing the past. (Photo by Wang Fuping)

During the 17th and 18th centuries in the Qing Dynasty, the tobacco and tea industries flourished in the southwest of Fujian. These commodities were sold all over the country and even overseas. With the development of the local economy and improvement of living standards, the need for improving residences became an urgent priority. At the same time, in order to safeguard the common interests of families, hundreds of clansmen chose to live together in the same building. Tulou of different shapes were built, with sizes becoming larger and larger due to increased wealth. Rich in diversity, with exquisite workmanship and gorgeous decorations, further enhanced by foreign culture, Fujian Tulou entered a stage of new heights.

After the 1950s, the local residents focused on improving the functionality of the Tulou, which led to simplified structures and decoration styles. This focus has continued on to today.

The existence of Tulou was known by very few until the mid-1950s when archeologists from home and abroad started studying them. In the early 1960s, Fujian Tulou attracted attention from American and Japanese scholars. After 1978 China's reform and opening up to the outside world encouraged more and more studies by foreigners regarding the Tulou. After 1982, experts from France, Peru, Belgium, Japan, as well as China's Hong Kong and Taiwan crowded to the Tulou for research. Since then, the people's enthusiasm in the Tulou has only been rising.

◎ 永定岩太土楼群。（王福平 摄）
Yantai Tulou Cluster in Yongding. (Photo by Wang Fuping)

1985年，联合国教科文组织顾问史蒂汶斯·安德烈（比利时籍）等一行，专程来永定考察土楼。安德烈赞叹："永定客家土楼是世界上独一无二的、神话般的山区建筑模式。"

2000年，国家历史文化名城保护专家委员会副主任郑孝燮考察永定土楼后赋诗一首，对土楼做出了准确概括和评价：

绝无仅有天地间，外如城堡内家园。

中原几度经战乱，聚族迁居千百年。

1998年至2008年，福建土楼所在地政府部门高度重视，为福建土楼的保护做了大量卓有成效的工作，经过10年的不懈努力，2008年7月7日，在加拿大魁北克城举行的第32届世界遗产大会上，"福建土楼"被正式列入《世界遗产名录》，福建土楼从此誉满天下。2008年11月，福建土楼被联合国教科文组织授予"遗产保护杰出成就奖"。

福建土楼如繁星般散落在闽西南的古老村落，历史源远流长、数量种类繁多、建筑规模宏大、多种功能齐全、文化底蕴深厚，在千姿百态的世界民居建筑中别具一格、独放异彩。它们融入自然、雄伟壮观、造型多样、布局规整、装饰华丽、聚族而居、安全防卫、舒适宜居，堪称建筑之瑰宝。

◎ 南靖田螺坑土楼群。（严孙锦 摄）
Tianluokeng Tulou Cluster in Nanjing.
(Photo by Yan Sunjin)

◎ 快乐的土楼孩子。（赖永生 摄）

The happy Tulou children. (Photo by Lai Yongsheng)

A team from the United Nations Educational, Scientific and Cultural Organization paid a special visit to the Tulou in 1985. Andrew Stevens, a UNESCO consultant from Belgium, spoke highly of the architecture, describing the Tulou as "a unique, fairytale-like architecture found nowhere else in the world".

Zheng Xiaoxie, the vice director of the Chinese National Committee of Experts on the Protection of Famous Historical and Cultural Cities wrote a poem on his visit to the Tulou in 2000:

> *One and the only one on earth,*
> *Fujian Tulou are like castles from outside and homeland inside.*
> *Survived from the wars on Central Plains,*
> *The Hakka people had migrated as a whole for thousands of years.*

From 1998 to 2008, the local government placed great importance on the protection of Tulou. The decade long effort in protecting the Tulou helped the architecture become part of the World Heritage List during the 32nd World Heritage Conference in Quebec City, Canada on July 7th, 2008. Since then, Tulou have gained much international coverage. In November 2008, Fujian Tulou were awarded the "Outstanding Achievement Award for Heritage Protection" by UNESCO.

Nestled amidst sprawling hills and winding mountain streams, the Tulou are renowned for their long history, great variety, large scale, delicate structure, rich cultural connotations and well-rounded functions. Merged with nature, the Tulou provided a comfortable and safe living space for the Hakka people.

融于自然　如画如诗

福建土楼建造的时候都是因地制宜，在合理安排房屋布局的同时，往往择址于依山傍水、青山绿水之间，楼与田园融为一体，构成一幅幅美丽的画卷。

"山上层层桃李花，云间烟火是人家"。在群山环抱中，土楼的四周是或山或水或田园，土楼人家可以在房屋的四周耕地种田、养鸡养鸭、放羊放牛、砍柴伐木、狩猎捕鱼，生产生活极其方便。蓝天白云下面，土楼背靠大山，远处有整整齐齐的绿竹、郁郁葱葱的森林，近处有层层拾级而上的梯田、满池荷叶的鱼塘。土楼与土楼之间却错落有致，鹅卵石铺成的小石路，木头扎成的小桥，在花花草草间曲径通幽。楼前屋后，桃树、李树、柿子树、柚子树、枇杷树、杨梅树、梨树，各种各样的果树林林总总。土楼冬无严寒，四季花开，桃花艳、梨花白、柿树红、梅香悠，土楼在红花绿叶之中若隐若现，有如仙山琼阁，美不胜收。有的土楼大门前，小溪边，散落着形态各异的大小石头，清澈的溪水或从小桥下面流过，或从石头之间流过。这般小桥流水人家的如诗如画的风景，可在福建土楼随处拾得。

◎ 永定新南村土楼。（胡家新 摄）
Two Tulou in Xinnan Village in Yongding. (Photo by Hu Jiaxin)

◎ 永定岩太村土楼。（胡家新 摄）

A Tulou in Yantai Village of Yongding. (Photo by Hu Jiaxin)

The Nature-Integrated Scenery

The Hakka ancestors arranged the Tulou's layout in line with the local conditions. Situated between mountains and streams, the Tulou blend in naturally, as if featured in an exquisite painting.

Right beside the Tulou are mountains, streams and farmlands. The residents live a self-sufficient life by cultivating land, breeding poultry, herding sheep and cattle, cutting firewood, hunting and fishing. Neat bamboo and lush green trees stand in the distance. Layers upon layers of terraced fields pair with the lotus-filled ponds. Peach, plum, persimmon, grapefruit, loquat, bayberry and pear trees bloom in spring, decorating the Tulou with flowers and leaves. Pebble paved country roads and wooden bridges connect various well-spaced Tulou. The murmuring brook in the green forest flows under the bridge and across the pebbles. Everything seems too beautiful to be real, even though it is common scenery around the Tulou.

© 永定高北荷色土楼。（胡家新 摄）

Tulou by a lotus-covered pond in Gaobei Tulou Cluster in Yongding. (Photo by Hu Jiaxin)

© 南靖上坂村。（冯木波 摄）
Shangban Village in Nanjing. (Photo by Feng Mubo)

气势磅礴　雄伟壮观

　　福建土楼数量多、分布广，其建筑规模气势非凡，蔚为壮观。每一座土楼大都在2层以上，最高的达到6层。有的村庄由几十座甚至上百座土楼组成。土楼那粗犷的石基以及高大的土墙，傲然矗立在世人面前，令人惊叹。

　　土楼占地从几千平方米至一万多平方米，楼高从3层到6层，房间数从几十到几百，从动工兴建到迁入居住耗时几年，甚至十几年、几十年，可以想象土楼规模之浩大、工程之艰巨。

　　大部分土楼的墙基深埋在地下用大块的山石干砌而成，高出地面50厘米以上的石墙基用稍小一些的石块砌筑，石墙基之上的土墙用泥土和一些毛竹片或杉树枝一并夯实。建造土楼的原材料取之于自然，又与大自然完美结合、浑然天成。一幢幢土楼昂然挺立于青山绿水之间，气势磅礴，质朴天然。

　　土楼先民因地取材、传承古老的夯墙技术，将原来松散的生土结合普普通通的一些材料，夯筑成历经千百年却依然高大坚固的土墙，不能不说是一个奇迹。

◎ 永定初溪土楼群中有着600年历史的集庆楼内景。（胡家新　摄）
The 600-year-old Jiqinglou in Chuxi Tulou Cluster in Yongding. (Photo by Hu Jiaxin)

◎ 南靖下坂村的裕昌楼倒影。（胡家新 摄）
Reflection of Yuchanglou in Xiaban Village of Nanjing. (Photo by Hu Jiaxin)

The Splendid Construction

The great number, wide distribution and large scale of Fujian Tulou make them extraordinary and magnificent. Most of the Tulou are above two storeys, and the highest has up to six storeys. Dozens or even hundreds of Tulou make up the villages. The rough stone foundation and the tall earth wall of the Tulou give it a splendid charm.

The construction of Tulou is arduous. Each Tulou can cover an area from one thousand to ten thousand square meters. The height is between three to six storeys and the number of rooms varies from dozens to hundreds. It takes several years for people to build and move into the Tulou.

Most Tulou foundations are made of large blocks of mountain stones, buried deep underground. Over 50 centimeters above the ground are stone foundations of the walls. Branches, strips of wood and bamboo chips are often laid in the wall as additional reinforcement. All the Tulou's building materials are sourced from nature. Among the hills and streams, the Tulou present their natural, pure and magnificent beauty.

The walls of each Tulou are strong and sturdy, standing as protection. It is a miracle that the Tulou, made of simple raw materials and by the most basic building techniques, have survived throughout centuries, living through bandit attacks and earthquakes.

造型多样　异彩纷呈

　　福建土楼千姿百态，外观造型多种多样，除了常见的方形和圆形，还有府第式等其他形状。早期的土楼多为方形，后出现圆形土楼和其他形状的土楼。从数量上看，方形土楼远远多于其他形状的土楼。

　　方形土楼简称"方楼"，主要有正方形和长方形土楼，而3至4层的正方形巨宅最为常见，少数多达5至6层。另有"一"字形、"回"字形、"日"字形、"目"字形等多种形态。底层为厨房、膳厅或客厅，二层为粮仓或卧室，三层及三层以上为卧室。楼中的天井为开放空间，有的楼各处高度相同，有的楼后部最高。土楼房间门多朝向天井，与走廊互相连通，厅堂则多在中轴线后端。

The Variety of Tulou Shapes

Fujian Tulou appear in various shapes. They are most commonly rectangular or circular, while some styles are more like traditional Chinese pavilions. The rectangular Tulou tend to be older and greater in number.

The rectangular Tulou, called Fanglou in Chinese, can be categorized more specifically into square, rectangle, the Yi (Chinese:一) shape, the Hui (Chinese:回) shape, the Ri (Chinese:日) shape, the Mu (Chinese:目) shape, and so on. Square monocyclic Tulou with three to four storeys are the most common, while some have five to six storeys. Kitchens and dining rooms are on the first floor, while the rooms on the second floor are used for storage or as bedrooms; those on the third level and above are bedrooms.

The courtyards are open spaces. The four walls of rectangular Tulou are usually of the same height; however, there are some that have a slightly higher back wall. Inside the entrance is a huge central courtyard which all the doors and windows of the rooms face. Corridors connect all the rooms and the hall is usually located towards the centre back of the building.

© 永定初溪土楼群鸟瞰。（胡家新 摄）
An aerial view of Chuxi Tulou Cluster in Yongding. (Photo by Hu Jiaxin)

◎ 位于永定高北土楼群的圆形土楼代表承启楼鸟瞰图。（冯木波 摄）
A bird's eye view of the typical circular Tulou Chengqilou in Gaobei Tulou Cluster in Yongding. (Photo by Feng Mubo)

　　圆形土楼是福建土楼中造型艺术最富魅力的一种。按其环数多少，可分为单环和多环两种，中间是宽阔的天井。单环圆楼一般只有两三层，最高的有5层。多环土楼规模更大，结构更复杂，整体性更强。福建土楼中的圆形土楼多为两环，如永定区湖坑镇振成楼就是其中的代表。环数最多的是永定区高头乡的承启楼，有4环，是现存最庞大、最有气势的大圆楼。虽然圆楼只占福建土楼的一小部分，但每一座圆楼都是生土建筑中的精品。

The circular Tulou are some of the most charming. There are two styles of circular Tulou: single-ringed or multi-ringed, with an open courtyard in the centre of each building. Most single-ringed Tulou have only two or three storeys, while some have five. The multi-ringed Tulou are larger in scale and more complex in structure, being united as a whole. The most commonly seen circular Tulou are of two rings, such as Zhenchenglou in Hongkeng Tulou Cluster, Hukeng Township of Yongding County as representative. Another multi-ringed Tulou is Chengqilou of Gaobei Tulou Cluster in Yongding County. It is a massive round Tulou with four concentric rings, being the biggest and the most complete and the most attractive round building in existence. Though the circular Tulou only account for a small part of the Tulou in Fujian, each of them is a precious example of stunning earthen construction.

　　五凤楼、府第式方楼、宫殿式方楼为数不多，显得有些特别。这三种土楼相似之处在于都有设厅堂，楼两侧为横楼。五凤楼主要以三堂为中轴核心，前低后高，逐级升高，屋脊5层叠，错落有致，整个外形犹如展翅欲飞的凤凰。府第式方楼层次不多，结构相对简单，装饰较为朴素。后楼为主楼，比前楼高2至3层。宫殿式方楼装饰精美、结构复杂，后面的建筑屋顶均比前楼及两侧的横楼屋顶高一层，逐级升高、层层叠叠、层次分明。

◎ 永定洪坑土楼群的福裕楼是五凤楼的典型代表。（赖永生 摄）
Fuyulou in Hongkeng Tulou Cluster of Yongding is a classic representation of pavilion style Tulou. (Photo by Lai Yongsheng)

While there are many styles of Tulou that can be found, there are few of the following styles: the phoenix style, the mansion style and the palace style. Their rarity makes them just a bit more special. These three styles of Tulou are similar in that they all have halls running down both sides. The phoenix style buildings are mainly composed of three halls at the centre and are low at the front and high at the back. Generally rising five storeys high, it looks like smaller homes stacked one on top another, making it look like a phoenix ready for flight.

The mansion style buildings do not have as many floors as the phoenix style buildings. The structure is often simple and decoration minimal. The main area which is located at the back is about two to three storeys higher than the section at the front of the building.

The palace style buildings are beautifully decorated and complex in structure. The roof at the back section rises higher than the front of the building. Long horizontal roofs line both sides and one can see all the different layers that create the whole building.

除了上述类型的土楼以外，福建还有许多富有特色的土楼，如多边形土楼、方圆结合形土楼、半月形土楼、阶梯形土楼等。

福建土楼群异彩纷呈，有的土楼成群成片，像皇宫的高墙大院，气势恢宏；有的方楼圆楼相间，错落别致；有的圆楼密布、环环相依……千姿百态的土楼群，点缀着闽西南山区的秀美山川，成为一道道亮丽的风景线。

Besides the above-mentioned styles of Tulou, there are many others which are characterized by various shapes such as polygonal, combined circle-square, crescents and terraced Tulou.

Many Tulou are built in concentrated groups, forming Tulou clusters here and there. Seen from the distance, some clusters look as magnificent as palaces. Fujian Tulou are well arranged in location, neither too dense nor too sparse. The combination of different styles of Tulou decorates the mountains and rivers in Fujian, presenting stunning countryside.

◎ 五角形楼顺源楼位于永定高东村，建于1839年。楼高三层，内院呈三角形，整个建筑顺应地势，自由布局，内部空间层次丰富而有变化，被誉为"最别致的土楼"。遗憾的是2018年毁于一场大火。（赖永生 摄）

Located in Gaodong Village of Yongding, Shunyuanlou was constructed in 1839 in a pentagonal shape. Standing three storeys high, it displays a triangular structure internally. It conforms to the topography of the land and has a flexible layout, making it known for its unique style. Regrettably, it was destroyed in a fire in 2018. (Photo by Lai Yongsheng)

◎ 位于永定南江村的八角形土楼东成楼，建楼时因周边有路和其他房子，遂削去四
个角而成八角形。（赖永生 摄）

Located in Nanjiang Village of Yongding, Dongchenglou is peculiar in that it is octagonal
shaped as a result of building it amongst the pre-existing roads and houses. (Photo by Lai
Yongsheng)

◎ 位于永定南江村前圆后方的D形土楼永宁楼。（赖永生 摄）

The D-shaped Yongninglou located in Nanjiang Village of Yongding. (Photo by Lai Yongsheng)

布局规整　严谨有序

　　福建土楼都有严谨有序的对称结构，每一座土楼都能找到一条鲜明的中轴线，连接大门—主楼—厅堂，横屋和其他附属建筑分布在左右两侧，呈对称格局。

　　土楼里最重要的部分是厅堂。厅堂的位置便是一座土楼的起点，也是全楼的中心，以厅堂为中心规划院落，再以院落为中心进行土楼整体的组合。厅堂是全楼的公共活动中心，土楼人在此举行祭祀祭拜、婚丧喜庆、家族议事、宴请宾客等重要活动。

　　楼内所有房间门都朝向楼内天井，都从楼内天井采光，各个房间鳞次栉比，组合成一个齐整有序的整体。门厅、天井、楼梯是全楼的公共部分。无论哪一种类型的土楼，都设有贯通全楼的回廊或通道，连接起各房间或各小院落。这些四通八达的廊道，不仅便于楼内居民的日常饮食起居，也便于楼内宗亲走动串门，沟通感情。

◎ 永定高北土楼群的世泽楼内景。
（胡家新 摄）

The interior of Shizelou in Gaobei Tulou
Cluster in Yongding. (Photo by Hu Jiaxin)

The Strict Layout

Fujian Tulou are consistent in their layout and construction. It is usually a central area surrounded by symmetrical wings. There is usually a central axis that runs from the entrance gate through the main building and then to the hall.

The key part of each Tulou is the hall, which represents the starting point and the centre of the whole building. The rest of the building tends to be planned around this centre. The hall is the place where the residents hold clan ceremonies, family meetings, wedding celebrations and funeral rites. Many other big events also take place in the hall, including hosting important guests.

The door of each room faces the Tulou's courtyard, allowing natural light to filter through the rooms. One by one, the rooms are closely arranged, being combined as a standardized and orderly whole. The public area includes the hall, the courtyard and the stairs. No matter what type of Tulou it is, there are corridors and public staircases which run through the whole building. Being accessible in all directions, the corridors help the residents communicate with each other.

◎ 永定洪坑土楼群振成楼内的精美内饰。（王福平 摄）

The exquisite interior of Zhenchenglou in Hongkeng Tulou Cluster in Yongding. (Photo by Wang Fuping)

装饰华丽　精致古朴

　　福建土楼大多进行了内部装饰，有的华丽精致，有的简约古朴，一般都布局在土楼的公共部位或显眼的地方。这些雕刻和绘画，不仅提升了土楼的文化价值，也透射出主人的文化修养与身份地位，彰显了土楼豪华的气派和深刻的内涵。

　　土楼内中厅的屏门、梁柱及镂窗上，可以看见精雕细刻、各具特色的木雕作品，有浮雕和镂空，有的还用镀金镶边。雕刻内容也丰富多彩，有花有草，有鸟有鱼，山水云海，亭台楼阁，但更多表现的是脍炙人口的传统故事，刀工细腻，线条流畅，人物栩栩如生。

　　土楼的梁柱之间有多种多样的木雕装饰，如狮子、祥龙、凤凰和其他鸟兽，以及莲花、松苞、葫芦等各种花木，各具神态、形象逼真。有的雕饰清新淡雅，有的"浓妆艳抹"，显得华丽夺目。

The Exquisite Workmanship of the Tulou

Fujian Tulou have generously decorated interiors. Many gorgeous, delicate and elaborate decorations are placed in the public area or other obvious places. The paintings and carvings not only enhance the aesthetic value of the building, but also embodies the owners' cultivation and social status. They present splendid styles and profound connotations.

Exquisite carvings are commonly seen on the screen doors and windows in the centre hall of the Tulou. The screen doors, made of hardwood, are carved with different techniques: some in relief or hollowed out while others are fringed with gold. In addition to an array of carvings of flowers, birds, fish, landscapes and pavilions, most carvings are of people and their stories.

On and between pillars and beams lie various wooden sculptures, vividly showing lions, dragons, phoenix and other birds and beasts, as well as flowers and trees including lotus, pine buds and gourds. Every piece is different from another. Some are even painted with bright colours, which makes them more dazzling.

◎ 永定下洋镇永康楼里的雕梁画栋。（张耀辉 摄）
Carved beams in Yongkanglou at Xiayang Township, Yongding. (Photo by Zhang Yaohui)

◎ 漳州平和县绳武楼里的槅扇。（胡家新 摄）
Sliding doors in Shengwulou in Pinghe County,
Zhangzhou. (Photo by Hu Jiaxin)

在土楼的楼门、石柱等处还有石雕、泥塑、彩塑等，其中以胶泥为坯、敷以五彩或彩色瓷片制成的装饰品具有较高的民间艺术价值。一些较大型的土楼中还可见到玻璃镶嵌的屏风、栏杆和镂窗等，与泥塑、彩塑相互呼应，让宏大的土楼庄严中多了些审美的细腻。

Stone sculptures, clay sculptures and coloured sculptures can also be found on the doors, pillars and pillar foundations of the Tulou. These demonstrate the folk carving technique which uses clay as the base and paints the sculptures with colours or covers them with porcelain pieces to make works of art. In some larger Tulou, coloured glass is carefully chosen to decorate screens, railings and windows. The beautiful sculptures bring more colours and vitality to the large buildings.

◎ 南靖怀远楼里的精美瓷窗。（冯木波 摄）
The porcelain window in Huaiyuanlou of Nanjing.
(Photo by Feng Mubo)

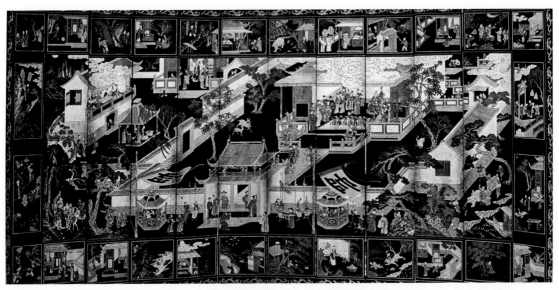

◎ 高北土楼群承启楼里的描金屏风。（王福平 摄）
A beautiful screen with gold foils in Chengqilou of Gaobei Tulou Cluster. (Photo by Wang Fuping)

　　在土楼还可以看到许许多多线条流畅、画风各异的壁画以及笔精墨妙的书法，颇有艺术特色。许多土楼的主人在门厅、天井、门坪等处用小鹅卵石砌成各种富有创意的精美图案。有的土楼还珍藏着做工精细、色彩鲜艳的屏风，极具欣赏价值。

Paintings and calligraphy can be frequently found hanging on the walls of the Tulou, showing much artistic merit. Some owners also decorate their hall, courtyard and doorway with pebbles placed in creative shapes and patterns. In some Tulou, collections of painted screens with fine workmanship and bright colours are also something to be appreciated.

◎ 精美的石雕、砖雕、木雕。（王福平 摄）
Delicate stone carving, brick carving and wood carving. (Photo by Wang Fuping)

◎ 其乐融融一家亲。（王福平 摄）
A happy communal life. (Photo by Wang Fuping)

聚族而居　其乐融融

　　土楼人有着特殊的聚族而居的生活方式，即同宗同族的许多家庭共同居住在一座土楼内，在各自拥有一定的私有财产、经济相对独立的同时，又有一些不可分割的共有财产，如田产、山林等。日常生活中有公共场所，如土楼的天井、厅堂、门坪等；生产中共用一些生产工具，如石磨、石舂、风谷机、打谷机等。对于一些祖宗留下来的不可分割的田产和山林，由同族德高望重、忠实正派的长者管理，获得的收入均用于土楼维护、修桥铺路等。

　　一座土楼就是一个家族的凝聚中心。一般的土楼住着数十上百人，规模宏大的住着数百人，多代同堂。有爷爷、奶奶、父母、叔伯、兄弟、侄子、妯娌、婆媳等宗亲关系。楼内每户人家地位平等，房间面积、数量相同，没有高低贵贱之分，只有公平公正和团结和谐。在兵荒马乱的年代，大家齐心协力，守卫家园。太平盛世则敦亲睦邻、互相帮助、其乐融融，蕴含着土楼同宗血缘的凝聚力。

The Particular Communal Living Style in the Tulou

Tulou people enjoy a special communal living style, where families of the same clan live together in the same Tulou. Each family has both private property, being relatively economically independent, and some indivisible common property, such as fields, mountains and forests. They also share public places like courtyards, halls, doorways and so on, as well as common tools of life and production, including stone mills, windmills, big stone motars and threshers. The elders with high moral values, loyalty and decency are in charge of the fields and forests left by the ancestors. The income is used for the maintenance of the Tulou including repairing bridges and paving roads.

Each Tulou serves as the cohesive centre of a clan. Although there are independent families in each Tulou, they fit together well and form a united whole. Hundreds of people can live in one Tulou, including grandparents, parents, brothers, uncles and nephews, mothers-in-law and daughters-in-law and other patriarchal relationships. Every family enjoys the same offerings of rooms and floor plans. Everyone is equal here. In the era of war and chaos, they worked together to defend themselves against the enemies. In a time of peace and order, the families help each other and work for the common goals, demonstrating the strong bond present in their blood lineage.

◎ 土楼墙下玩游戏的孩子们。（胡家新 摄）
Tulou children are playing games. (Photo by Hu Jiaxin)

防火防盗　巧夺天工

　　巨大的福建土楼具有巧夺天工的安全防卫功能。这是因为大部分土楼都有3层以上，底层一般不开窗户。土楼墙厚一般在1米左右，有的甚至有2米多厚。

　　土楼一、二层大多是厨房和谷仓，所以一二层的外墙几乎都不开窗户，除了防潮，更能防止强盗土匪从窗口爬入楼内。大门门框用厚重、坚硬的花岗石条或青石条砌成，门板则是用十多厘米厚的硬木板制成，有的还包上一层铁皮，门闩是一根或多根粗壮的方柱形硬木头。大门的门顶过梁上方墙中埋入竹筒作水槽或沙槽，水槽或沙槽与门厅二层楼上的水箱相连。一旦大门遭遇火攻，可以立即用水或沙子灭火。

　　土楼内的廊道上下连通、四通八达，全楼每个角落都畅通无阻。许多土楼还在顶层的四面建筑瞭望台或者瞭望窗，这些瞭望台（窗）在动荡不安的年代可以观察楼外的动静以及打击进犯的敌人，在和平年代则作为观景台，俯瞰土楼外面的秀丽风光。

◎ 高大厚实的外墙，可作瞭望台的小窗。
（王福平 摄）
Thick walls with small windows which could be used as lookouts. (Photo by Wang Fuping)

◎ 损毁的古老土楼，大门依然坚固。（胡家新 摄）

The strong gate of an old damaged Tulou. (Photo by Hu Jiaxin)

The Massive Structures of Defense

The massive buildings are solid and constructed to efficiently defend the residents. Most of the buildings are from three to five storeys high, with no window on the ground floor, which prevents thieves and bandits. The earth packed walls of the Tulou are very thick, generally reaching 1 meter, or sometimes 2 meters thick.

The only entrance door is protected by hard granite or bluestone bars which are firmly implanted into the walls and the ground. The door made of rigid wood is framed with iron boards to prevent fire and attack. One or more pieces of thick tetragonal wood are used to bar and lock the door. Some bamboo tubes are embedded in the ceiling of the ground floor as water or sand channels, which are connected with the water tank above the door. If invaders or burglars were to set fire to the door, water or sand would flow down from the tank and put out the fire immediately.

The corridors in the Tulou extend to all directions, enabling every corner of the building easily accessible. On the top floor of some Tulou, there are lookouts on all sides. They were used to observe the situation outside the building and attack invading enemies in turbulent times. Now they are used as viewing decks or windows for residents to enjoy the surrounding scenery.

◎ 瞭望台和射击孔。（王福平 摄）
The lookout and firing ports.
(Photo by Wang Fuping)

◎ 大门上的防火水箱。（赖永生 摄）
The water tank over the entrance gate.
(Photo by Lai Yongsheng)

　　土楼木构件多，为了防止失火时火势迅速蔓延，一般从土楼的一层到顶层筑有带有门洞、不妨碍人们通行的防火墙。土楼的楼板用杉木或松木铺好以后，还需在上面铺一层青砖，不仅具有隔音和防尘的效果，还具有灭火的功能，万一发生火灾，楼板着火炭化以后，青砖在重力的作用下会和炭化的楼板一起往下掉，从而压灭火焰，遏制火势蔓延。此外，为了防火，有些土楼还会准备一些防火设施和用具，如在楼内打水井，既可解决居民日常饮水，又可满足灭火的不时之需。

　　在动荡不安的年代，面对如此厚实坚固、防卫功能强大的土楼，前来入侵的敌人总是无可奈何，土匪强盗更是望楼兴叹。哪怕敌人在土楼外面攻上十天半个月，甚至几个月，土楼居民也能充分利用土楼猪圈里的生猪、粮仓内的存粮以及鸡鸭、井水等坚持下来。

Firewalls with escape doors were built in each Tulou to prevent fires from rapidly spreading since there are so many wooden components in the Tulou. The wooden floors are usually covered with a layer of black brick. Besides the function of sound insulation and dust proofing, the black bricks can also stop the fire from spreading by falling down and putting out the flame. In addition, some Tulou are equipped with fireproofing facilities such as wells within the walls. They not only provide daily drinking water for residents, but also meet the occasional need for firefighting.

In front of such solid Tulou with such skillful defensive design, invaders or burglars could only find themselves in the mire. Even in cases where they may be under siege for as long as several months, because of the pigpen, granary, poultry and easy access to well water, the residents have the capabilities to sustain daily life.

◎ 土楼里的水井。（赖永生 摄）
The well inside a Tulou.
(Photo by Lai Yongsheng)

冬暖夏凉　舒适宜居

　　福建土楼依山傍水，既分散又集中，楼与楼之间错落有致，楼外几乎都有一个很开阔的门坪，楼内有宽敞的主天井和各个院落的小天井，这些都为楼内提供了足够的通风、采光条件。寒冬，田野出现了霜降或结冰，但只要关上所有的门窗，土楼用生土夯筑成的高大厚实的外墙和隔墙，便可把寒流挡在楼外。炎夏，青山绿水中的土楼，山风习习、溪风徐来，打开门窗，门与门、窗对窗形成空气对流，加上土楼厚厚的外墙起着隔热作用，楼内顿觉清凉，这时土楼的居民便成群聚集到巷道或门口，一边聊天，一边纳凉。

　　土楼厚实的墙体不仅有良好的隔热、防寒的功效，还有较强的吸水性能，当空气中的湿度大于墙体的湿度时，墙体自然而然地把空气中的水分吸收进去，从而降低楼内尤其是房间内的湿度；而当空气中的湿度小于墙体的湿度时，墙体里的水分则不断散发出来。墙体像湿度平衡器一样，自动调节着楼内的湿度。所以，土楼里面很少见到其他乡村常见的回潮现象，也在一定程度上保护楼内的楼板、楼梯等木制品不被虫蛀。

　　土楼楼内的排水系统也是设计巧妙，屋檐的滴水处深挖排水沟，使雨水往外流走，天井的平面向周围稍有倾斜，使楼内的积水能够及时通过排水沟排到楼外。有的土楼里面，排水沟里还能看到几只爬来爬去的乌龟，这些乌龟自由自在地生活在排水沟里，扮演着埋在地下的排水沟里的"疏通工"呢。

◎ 天井是居民谈天说地的聚集地。（王福平 摄）
The courtyard provides the residents a get-together place. (Photo by Wang Fuping)

◎ 土楼冬日。（王福平 摄）
A winter day in the Tulou.
(Photo by Wang Fuping)

The Comfortable and Liveable Life

The spacious main courtyard and small courtyards of the Tulou provide a well-lit, well-ventilated, and windproof area for the residents. It is much warmer inside the Tulou in winter since the tall and thick earth walls block the chilly wind from the fields. In summer, the inside temperature is lower than the outside temperature when the cooling wind passes through the building once all windows and doors of the Tulou are open. On summer evenings, residents always gather in groups around the gate. They like to talk about the events around the village while enjoying the gentle breeze.

The thick walls of the Tulou are not only efficient in heat insulation, but also have strong water absorbency. They naturally absorb the moisture in the air when the rooms are humid and emit the moisture when it is dry. This keeps the inside of the building neither too dry nor too damp. Besides, the floors, stairs, beams and columns of the Tulou are made of Chinese fir wood, which remains in a good state even when exposed to moisture and worms over years. No matter the season, the moisture will not build up in the Tulou as it commonly would in the countryside.

The drainage system in the Tulou is also ingeniously designed. Drainage ditches are dug under where water flows off the eaves, making the rain flow outward. The slightly slanted courtyard also helps drain the water out. In some ditches of the Tulou, there even live several turtles, crawling through and dredging the pipe.

土楼不土　建造独特

　　从一筐土到一面墙再到一座土楼，都凝聚了福建土楼先民的集体智慧，见证了福建土楼经历数百年无数次的地震撼动、风雨侵蚀而安然无恙的奇迹。福建土楼是世界民居建筑的一朵奇葩，被世人称为"东方古城堡"。

　　土楼建造工艺有多道工序，包括选址设计、请工备料、开基砌石、夯筑土墙、立柱安梁、屋顶施工、装饰装修等。各个工序有许多细致的步骤，每个步骤又要根据天气等各种实际情况巧妙施工。

■ 选址设计

　　旧时建土楼，选址是一个很复杂的过程，既要考虑传统易经的风水因素，也要考虑地形地貌等地理情况。另外，避风、向阳、减湿等等宜居要素都是选址时必须兼顾的。选好楼址以后，建楼的主人会请来风水先生、木匠师傅、泥水师傅等，一起商议谋划建房的有关事项，对土楼的形状、大小、高度、房间数量、土楼朝向、土墙厚度及内部设计等形成大致的思路。旧时没有设计图纸，但是这些能工巧匠们都能够对设计方案了然于胸。

The Unique Construction Process

From starting with a basket of earth to finishing a wall and then the whole building, every step of the Tulou construction process condenses the collective wisdom of the ancestors. Still standing through hundreds of years of earthquakes, wind and rain erosion, Fujian Tulou are considered miraculous global dwellings.

Known as the "Oriental Ancient Castle" by the world, the Tulou have a complex construction process as follows.

■ Choosing a Location

The site selection of the Tulou was a very complicated process back in the old days. It included considerations of traditional elements of the geomantic theory and scientific elements of landform, geography and landscape, such as shelter from wind, sunshine, dehumidification and so on. After the site was chosen, a Feng Shui master and the leading carpenter and plasterer were invited to discuss about the construction details, such as the height and size of the Tulou, the number of rooms.

■ 请工备料

　　建楼的良辰吉日确定以后，楼主人便要开始精心准备建造土楼所需的材料，包括生土、石料、木料、竹料、石灰、砖瓦等，这些材料大部分就近取材，取之不尽。有些材料要提前组织人员加工好，有的材料可以边施工边进料。材料准备好以后，就要邀请建楼的工人，除了之前请的风水先生、木匠师傅、泥水师傅外，还要请打石师傅、夯墙师傅、烧砖瓦师傅及后勤杂工等。客家人素有互相帮助的传统，只要有人家建造土楼，左邻右舍或者亲朋好友都会很主动过来帮忙，帮着运土、挑土上墙或做好后勤。

　　建楼前工作准备就绪，便等良辰吉日正式动工，一般动工时间都会选择下半年雨季过后。动工当天，要举行传统的开工仪式，楼主人要焚香祭拜天地祖先。这种古老的开工仪式充满了对祖先的追思、对大自然的敬畏。

◎ 准备木梁。（张耀辉 摄）

Making beams. (Photo by Zhang Yaohui)

◎ 备好生土。（张耀辉 摄）
Getting the earth ready. (Photo by Zhang Yaohui)

■ Preparing Materials and Hiring Labourers

The first thing to do when building a Tulou is to prepare materials and hire labourers. The labourers range from Feng Shui masters, masons, carpenters, plasterers, bricklayers, bamboo strips craftsmen, delivery men and back men, all of whom are experienced in their own field. Helping each other is a tradition of the Hakka people. As long as a family is building a Tulou, the neighbours, relatives and friends will come to help, carrying earth, ramming the walls, and providing supporting service. The main materials needed for building Tulou include raw earth, stone, wood, bamboo, lime, bricks and tiles. Some of these should be prepared before the construction starts, and others can be replenished while the construction is underway.

The construction begins with a grand sacrificial rite at a good time in the almanac, generally in the second half of the year. The builders burn incenses to worship the gods and ancestors. This ceremony shows Hakka people's respect to their ancestors as well as their awe to nature.

■ 开挖基沟

夯筑土楼时，要先在选定的楼址上，根据设计的土楼类型和底层开间数量及房间的大小，用石灰画出石脚线，这叫"牵石脚线"（也叫放样）。画好石脚线后，便开始挖墙基，墙基的深度和宽度要根据土楼的楼层来决定，楼越高墙基就要越宽、越深，如果土质松软，还要打上木桩，确保墙基牢固。三层以上的大型土楼的墙基比较坚实，一般在2至3米厚，深度在3米左右。

■ Excavating Ditches

Before ramming the walls, the builders should firstly draw some lines on the ground with lime under the guidance of the Feng Shui masters, based on the style of the Tulou, the number of the rooms and the space of each room. After marking the lines, the builders would dig pits with widths and depths that depended on the height of the building, the thickness of the earth walls and the soil quality of the foundation. The higher the building, the greater the load on a wider and deeper foundation. When it comes to soft ground, it is necessary to dig some wood post deep into the solid layer. The wall foundation of a large Tulou with over two floors is relatively solid, generally 2 to 3 meters thick and 3 meters deep.

◎ 忙碌的建楼女人。（张耀辉 摄）
Hard-working Tulou women. (Photo by Zhang Yaohui)

■ 砌筑石基

墙基挖好以后，就要在石脚坑内铺放石基。石基是土楼稳固的基础，分上下两层，埋在地下看不见的石基称大脚，露出地面的墙基称小脚。

大脚多以底面较平的大石块干砌，呈立体梯形状，下面大上面小，缝隙以小石块填紧，方土楼四角用整块巨石镇定，以确保屋角地基的稳定，边缘还要填土夯实。

小脚的厚度一般比墙体小4至5厘米，里外各缩进2厘米左右，这样比笔直的外墙更加美观。小脚以表面比较平的石块垒砌，石块的铺排必须与大脚石块的方向不同，这样才能稳固。小脚通常以三合土（石灰、黄泥、沙子按照一定比例拌和）湿砌，其砌法为石砌内外两层，接缝处必须错位，中间用小石块、三合土湿浆填实。墙角的小脚用较大块石片或者大方青砖砌成标准直角。石基的高度根据地基的土质来定，露出地面的石基一般在50厘米到100厘米之间，以免土墙受潮或被山洪冲蚀。

■ Constructing Stone Foundations

When the pits are ready, it is time to place the stones in to build the foundation. The stone foundations are key to the solidness of the Tulou, and consist of two layers: the lower layer buried underground is called Dajiao (Big Foot) and the upper called Xiaojiao (Small Foot).

Dajiao is mostly built with large stones with a flat bottom and is in the shape of a three-dimensional trapezium. This means the bottom of Dajiao is wider than the top. The cracks are filled with small stones. For the square Tulou, four whole giant stones are used in each corner of the foundation with compacted earth to ensure stability.

The thickness of Xiaojiao is generally 4 to 5 centimeters less than the wall, about 2 centimeters thinner from both inside and outside than the wall, which has a better appearance than a straight wall line. Xiaojiao is built by piling flat stones placed in different directions from the big stones in Dajiao. Mixed soil of lime, yellow mud and sand is used to fix the stones in the outer and inside layer of the wall. The gaps between the stones should be filled with small stones and wet mixed soil. The Xiaojiao at the corner is shaped into standard right angles with large stone pieces or bricks. The height of most Xiaojiao is over 50 centimeters to protect the earth walls from water, while some Xiaojiao reach nearly 100 centimeters high in case of flooding.

◎ 地基完工。（冯木波 摄）
The completed stone foundations. (Photo by Feng Mubo)

■ 夯筑土墙

　　小脚砌成，一般需要等20天左右三合土墙面干固之后，再开始夯筑土墙（也叫行墙），这是建造土楼最重要的工序。因此，行墙前要先准备好几项工作。一是需要做熟一批墙泥，墙泥最好是田底土（俗称"田隔泥"）或山脚红土，适当掺入细砂和水，用锄头反复翻动搅拌，直至土质和干湿度均匀。比较重要部位的墙泥，还必须将泥堆成土墩，拍打结实后，再削下来，有些要三打三削。二是要备足作墙骨的毛竹片或杉木条，这些唾手可得的材料需要放置两三年干透了方可使用。三是请木匠师傅提前做好门排和窗排。

　　行墙前一夜，楼主人都要请泥水匠师傅、木匠师傅、夯墙师傅、风水先生和帮工的左邻右舍好吃好喝一顿，让大家尽兴为止。

◎ 起土。（赖永生 摄）

Mixing the earth. (Photo by Lai Yongsheng)

◎ 夯墙。（张耀辉 摄）
Ramming the earth.
(Photo by Zhang Yaohui)

■ Ramming Earth Walls

It is time for the builders to rest for a few days after the Xiaojiao has been completed. The earth walls cannot be tamped until the mixed soil surface becomes dry and solid. The director of the construction always reminds the builders to do three things well since the wall tamping is the key process in building a Tulou. First, to prepare enough soil which contains certain sands. The best options are the soil coming from below the plowed soil in the field or at the foot of the mountain. Based on the soil quality, the builders would mix the soil with some sand and water, and turn it over and over with a hoe to make good plaster. The plaster for important parts of the Tulou should firstly be piled into a mound and tamped hard, then cut down to pieces. Some people may even repeat these processes three times. For the first and second floors of the Tulou which are built on low-lying land, slaked lime is added into the plaster for protection against flood and moisture.

The second task is to prepare enough bamboo slices and fir branches. As the Tulou are located in an area with vast forests, these materials are readily available. They are usually set aside for three years before they are thoroughly dry. Thirdly, the carpenters should make the doors and windows in advance.

The night before the ramming process, the owner of the building will invite the masons, carpenters, wall rammers, Feng Shui masters and his neighbours for a good meal and everyone enjoys themselves.

◎ 行墙。（张耀辉 摄）
Tamping the wall. (Photo by Zhang Yaohui)

　　行墙当天，主人要置办供品，祭拜天神、土地神，燃放鞭炮。夯墙的主要工具是用两块长2米左右的杉木板和挡板、墙板卡组成的墙枋。行墙开始时，将墙枋架在两根圆棍上，用墙板卡锁紧，形成一个固定的空间，倒入墙泥，夯墙师傅各执一杆舂杵，分立在墙板的两端，先铺土、踩平，再开始夯筑。一层夯实后再覆盖一层墙泥，一版墙需要夯实四层土才能完成。

　　倒入第三层土的时候，要放进称为"墙筋"的毛竹片或杉树枝，和泥土一并夯实。毛竹片或杉树枝坚硬而富有弹性，而且埋入土墙后与空气隔绝，不仅不会腐朽，还能起到钢筋一样的牵拉作用，在一定程度上达到防震防塌的效果。个别家境殷实、资金雄厚的人家考虑到第一版墙是最重要的承重墙，为防止岁月风化和人为的磨损会适当掺入一些红糖、糯米，从而起到更加坚固的作用。

　　每夯筑完一层楼的土墙，夯墙师傅都要检查质量，及时修墙补墙，确保每版墙枋筑出的土墙之间衔接良好、墙面紧密均匀、墙体结实。夯筑到适当的位置，还要放置门排和窗排。

On the day of ramming the wall, the owners worship the gods of heaven and earth, and will set off firecrackers. Two parallel wood boards are fixed on two horizontal logs where two rammers stand by. They put earth in between the boards and compact it until it becomes hard, then place another layer of earth and ram, repeating the process four times. When it comes to the third layer, a few pieces of bamboo slices or China fir branches should be buried in the earth, serving as the concrete iron. Some rich families would mix some glutinous rice and brown sugar with the earth so that the walls could last longer. The bamboo slices or Chinese fir branches embedded in the wall are isolated from the air, so they do not decay for hundreds of years. Moreover, they are hard but elastic. Even if the building leans due to earthquakes or other reasons, these materials in the walls will be pulled straight, helping the building stand still.

Every time a concrete wall is built, the rammers must check the quality and ensure all the walls are well connected, even and uniform so that it may stand strong. Not only that, door frames and window sills must be placed in appropriate positions.

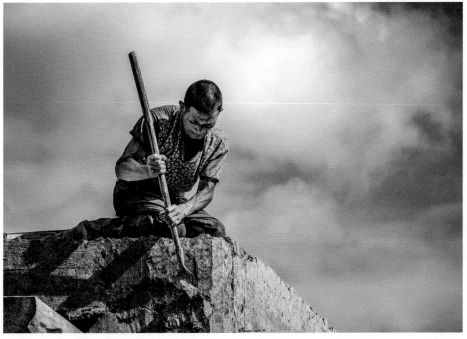

◎ 修墙角。（张耀辉 摄）
Fixing the corner of walls. (Photo by Zhang Yaohui)

◎ 上大梁。（胡家新 摄）
Installing the ridgepole.
(Photo by Hu Jiaxin)

■ 立柱安梁

　　每夯好一层楼高的土墙，木匠师傅便开始在土楼内侧立柱竖木，在木柱上架横梁，再在横梁和外围土墙之间铺设龙骨，形成房间和走廊的框架。龙骨上再铺木楼板，并用不会锈蚀的竹钉固定。因为土墙干透之后会因收缩降低高度，为了保持楼板水平，龙骨架在土墙的一端会适当抬高。

　　随着夯墙工序完成，楼墙高高耸起，最重要的安梁仪式也到来了。安放楼顶的栋梁之前，要在栋梁上油上红漆，画上八卦并裹上红布，悬挂五谷包。用五牲（鸡、鸭、猪、羊和鱼）三素（黑大豆、红糖果、甜糯米汤丸）祭梁。祭梁毕，泥水师傅、木匠师傅便用绳子拴住栋梁的两端，一层一层地吊到屋顶上，用水平尺测平，安放稳当，即完成安梁这道工序。安梁完成，点燃鞭炮，在鞭炮声中慢慢把墙枋放到地面，寓意历时已久的夯筑终于完工。

■ Making Frames

When the wall is built to the height of one floor, it is the time to make frames of the building. First, place pillars over the stone bases. Then place beams on the top of the pillars to make a frame of the whole floor. Between the beams and the outside walls are wooden columns which connect the corridor railings. Wooden boards are fixed on the columns to make floors with bamboo nails which never get rusty.

When it comes to the top floor, a ceremony is held before installing the important ridgepole. It is painted red with the eight diagrams, then wrapped in red cloth and worshiped with a chicken, a duck, a pig, a sheep, a fish, some black beans, red candies and sweet dumplings made of glutinous rice. Then it is lifted up and fixed on the top. This is then followed by setting off firecrackers and putting down the ramming model.

◎ 铺设屋顶。（张耀辉 摄）
Placing tile trusses. (Photo by Zhang Yaohui)

屋顶施工

屋顶对于生土夯筑的土楼来说至关重要。屋顶施工包括屋面钉桷板、盖瓦和处理排水、隔热、通风等工序。桷板一般3厘米厚度、12厘米宽，用杉木板制成，不易腐烂。盖瓦是土楼主体工程的最后一道工序。泥水师傅手持青瓦，蹲着从屋檐口开始盖瓦，盖好一片，就朝屋脊方向后退，直至屋脊，然后以青砖、石灰作屋栋，以防瓦片被风吹走或者漏雨。

屋顶排水施工时要在内外屋檐口下钉一块经过油漆的木板，不让雨水倒灌进来。隔热通风处理则主要是在土楼顶部建筑顶棚或阁楼，或在瓦顶下面的承重土墙上开挖缺口、通风窗。

Installing the Roof

After installing the ridgepole, other beams and tile trusses will be put in place. The tile trusses should be placed parallel to the beams at an interval of about 0.7 to 1 meter. Then along the slope of the front and back roof, Chinese fir boards are nailed based on the roof's size. Then they are covered with tiles. The roof is generally skillfully designed for preventing rainwater, insulating heat and ventilating.

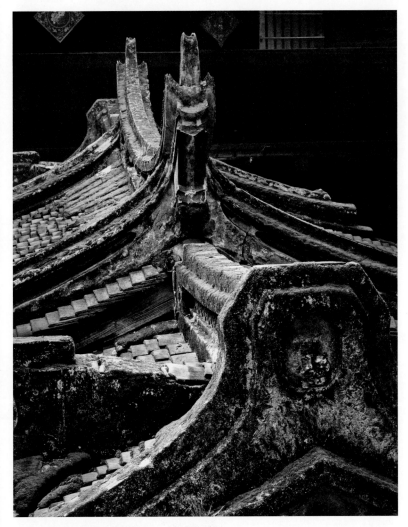

◎ 永定洪坑土楼群奎聚楼屋顶。（胡家新 摄）
Part of the roofs of Kuijulou in Hongkeng Tulou Cluster in Yongding. (Photo by Hu Jiaxin)

◎ 屋顶上的细节装饰。（赖永生 摄）

Decorations on the roofs. (Photo by Lai Yongsheng)

■ 装饰装修

　　土楼建成干透，可能长达数年的装修便拉开了帷幕。泥水师傅要开挖窗口、砌泥砖墙、铺设天井、铺砌地面、砌排水沟、建灶。木匠师傅则要安装楼梯、安装楼门、铺楼板、做走廊栏杆以及门窗等等。石工师傅要打造土楼通道、门坪、天井、水井、石柱、门框及厅廊地面等需要的石料。雕饰师傅在门、窗、隔、屏、檐、梁等处描绘出许多形象栩栩如生、纹样精美绝伦的雕饰精品。这些能工巧匠们在土楼装修装饰中把自己高超的技艺发挥得淋漓尽致。装修结束后，一座土楼终于建成。楼主人挑选良辰吉日，乔迁新居。

　　土楼多在秋冬农闲之时动工兴建。每天连续夯筑土墙的高度没有定数，而且要留有足够的风干期，须干到一定程度后才能再加高。大型土楼一般夯到一层楼的高度时，就要停工一些时日，待土墙自然干燥压实后才能继续夯。因此，建造一座土楼，短则一两年，长则需要十几年甚至几十年，凝结着几代人的心血。有人形容道，"一生半座楼，一楼几代人"。

■ Decoration

When the building is thoroughly dry, decorating begins and may last for several years. The plasterers excavate windows, build mud and brick walls, pave the courtyard and ground, dig drainage ditches and build cookstoves. The carpenters build stairs, cover the floors, build corridor railings, doors and windows. The masonries make stones for the corridors, doors, courtyards, water wells, pillars, doorframes and floors of the hall. The sculptors give full play to their skills, carving vivid and exquisite features in doors, windows, partitions, screens, eaves and beams. When all these are finished, the owners of the building choose a good day in the almanac to move in, and start their life in their new home.

Construction of the Tulou generally begins in autumn and winter when there is less farm work. There is no fixed height of the wall required for every day. Enough air-drying time should be allowed before the walls can be built higher. When a large Tulou is tamped to the height of one floor, the construction work may stop for some time. The tamping cannot continue until the earth wall is naturally dried and compacted. Therefore, the construction of a Tulou takes from one or two years to more than ten years or even decades, consisting of the efforts of several generations.

◎ 精心装饰的厅堂。（赖永生 摄）
A well-decorated hall. (Photo by Lai Yongsheng)

土楼神韵——异彩纷呈的古老城堡

　　福建土楼数以万计，或"成群结队"，形成土楼村、土楼沟、土楼"长城"；或"孤傲独居"，散落在闽西南崇山峻岭之中。成千上万座土楼，因地形、条件或风水所限，形成了除方楼、圆楼、五凤楼以外的多边形楼，包括五角楼、六角楼、八角楼、"日"字形楼、"吕"字形楼、"富"字形楼等等，显得那样千姿百态、丰富多彩。

　　2008年7月，福建土楼中有46座土楼被正式列入《世界遗产名录》，其中包括龙岩市永定区"三群两楼"（指初溪土楼群、洪坑土楼群、高北土楼群和振福楼、衍香楼），漳州市南靖县"两群两楼"（指田螺坑土楼群、河坑土楼群与和贵楼、怀远楼），以及漳州市华安县的大地土楼群。

　　走进千百年人文积淀的土楼，轻轻抚摸里面的每一扇门、每一扇窗、每一面墙，你都能深深感受到土楼博大精深的文化和神奇的故事，惊叹于土楼居民的勤劳与智慧。你也可以静静地蹲在土楼里面的阴阳水井旁，或坐在那历经数百年风雨洗礼的石板凳上，真真切切感受土楼里生生不息的脉动，感受她令人着迷的魅力。她的神秘与美丽，总会让你念念不忘，回味无穷。

Enchanting Tulou: Splendid Castles

There are tens of thousands of Tulou scattered in the mountains of southwestern Fujian. Their shapes have been influenced by terrain, Feng Shui and weather conditions. As a result, there are many more polygonal shaped buildings in addition to the square, circular and pagoda like ones mentioned here today.

In July 2008, forty-six of the numerous Fujian Tulou buildings were officially inscribed on the UNESCO World Heritage List. From Yongding District of Longyan, there is Chuxi Tulou Cluster, Hongkeng Tulou Cluster, Gaobei Tulou Cluster, Zhenfulou and Yanxianglou. From Nanjing County of Zhangzhou, there is Tianluokeng Tulou Cluster, Hekeng Tulou Cluster, Heguilou and Huaiyuanlou. Finally, in Hua'an County, Zhangzhou, the Dadi Tulou Cluster.

Rich with ancient human history, a gentle touch across every door, every window and every wall of the Tulou can make you feel a deep sense of profound culture as well as the magical story behind these earthen dwellings. It is a moment to connect with the hard work and wisdom of the Tulou's residents. Calmly reflect next to the wells that represent Yin and Yang, or sit on the stone bench which has stood strong through all weather conditions for centuries. It is a time to truly appreciate the energy and the charm of the Tulou. Their mystery and beauty will always find a place in your fondest memories.

◎ 永定初溪土楼群的初春。
（胡家新 摄）
Early spring in Chuxi Tulou Cluster in Yongding. (Photo by Hu Jiaxin)

永定初溪土楼群

　　初溪土楼群（初溪土楼古村落）位于龙岩市永定区下洋镇初溪村，距离永定城区47千米。初溪土楼群整体坐南朝北，背靠海拔1,200多米的高山。站在位于北面山上的初溪村观景台上登高俯瞰，整个初溪土楼群尽收眼底，层层叠叠，错落有致，其磅礴的气势令人震撼。土楼群的后面及两边是层层梯田，山顶上的周边还有几座若隐若现的土楼。从远处眺望，初溪土楼群以及这个传统古村落就在云雾之中显得那么神秘那么充满魅力。其中最引人注目的是"三圆一方"的土楼景观，它们由东向西依次排列，分别是初溪土楼群中最大最古老的四座土楼：余庆楼、庚庆楼、集庆楼和绳庆楼。

　　初溪土楼群依山而建，临水而居。从四座土楼往下走过约20多米长的石头路，便是一条自东向西潺潺流动的小溪。小溪清澈见底，高出水面的几个桥墩般的石块，便是村民们过往小溪的天然"石桥"了。从一个石墩轻轻地跨到另一个石墩，聆听脚下哗哗的流水声，踩上那条饱经沧桑的石砌路，顿时感受到土楼、流水、石砌路以及山川田野、蓝天白云融为一体的亘古韵味。

　　初溪土楼群规模宏大，类型丰富，有长方形、正方形、圆形、椭圆形、八角形等多种外形，显得生动而立体。其中被列入《世界遗产名录》的土楼就有集庆楼、庚庆楼、余庆楼、绳庆楼、善庆楼、锡庆楼、共庆楼、福庆楼、华庆楼、藩庆楼共10座土楼。它们大多保存完好，至今还保留着原有的建筑格局，具有较高的历史价值、建筑学价值和艺术价值。因此，初溪土楼群成为福建土楼申报世界文化遗产的重要组成部分。

　　初溪土楼群有五个最，即最集中、最美丽、最古老、最完整、最知名；有"五个一"的独特特点，即"一种姓，一朝向，一道门，一个庆，无一井"，这里的土楼主人都姓徐，所有楼都坐南朝北。因为风水和防御的原因，土楼均只有一个朝北开的门户。楼前就有用之不竭的潺潺溪水，故而所有楼内都不打水井。600多年来，大部分土楼均用"庆"字命名。或许正是徐氏先人追求"升平雅乐、温良善德"的生活，在他们心里，"庆"字蕴含着"喜庆、吉祥"的意思，寓意徐氏族人代代相传，人丁兴旺，吉祥如意。

　　初溪土楼群反映了自然山水和村落历史环境有机结合的杰出风貌，在山势陡峭、地形复杂的大山深处形成了颇为壮观的与大自然融为一体的土楼群村落，是人与自然完美结合、和谐相处的典范。

　　初溪土楼群所在的初溪村，2014年11月被列入第三批"中国传统村落"名录。它见证了客家古村落发展的历史过程，保留了福建土楼的真实自然和原始特征。

◎ 永定初溪土楼群。（王福平 摄）
Chuxi Tulou Cluster in Yongding. (Photo by Wang Fuping)

Chuxi Tulou Cluster in Yongding

Chuxi Tulou Cluster (also known as Chuxi Tulou Ancient Village) is located 47 kilometres away from the downtown, in Chuxi Village, Xiayang Town, in Yongding District of Longyan. Facing the north, the Tulou in the village are neighbours to mountains that tower at 1,200 metres in height. On the north face of the mountain is an observation deck. From here one can take in the panoramic views of Chuxi Tulou Cluster with all its majestic glory. A few Tulou buildings are nestled between terraced fields and the mountain face. Looking at it from a distance, Chuxi Tulou Cluster lives up to its description of being an ancient yet mysterious village that sits within the clouds. The most striking points of focus are the four largest and oldest Tulou buildings of the cluster: three circular and one square shaped Tulou. These are Yuqinglou, Gengqinglou, Jiqinglou and Shengqinglou.

◎ "三圆一方"由左向右依次为余庆楼、庚庆楼、集庆楼、绳庆楼。（王福平 摄）
Left to right: Yuqinglou, Gengqinglou, Jiqinglou and Shengqinglou (the square one). (Photo by Wang Fuping)

Chuxi Tulou Cluster was built on the hillside close to flowing water. Walking down a twenty-metre-long path down from the Tulou will bring you to a crystal-clear stream flowing from east to west. Several stones protruding out above the water form a natural stone bridge for villagers to cross the stream. Hopping from one stone to another, listen to the sound of the running water under your feet. Savour the pristine moment as a sense of appreciation for the ancient earthen buildings, the movement of the water, the stony paths, the mountains, the fields and the white clouds in the blue sky washes over you.

Comparatively large and vast in designs, Chuxi Tulou Cluster consists of rectangular, square, elliptical, and octagonal shaped buildings. Among these structures are Jiqinglou, Gengqinglou, Yuqinglou, Shengqinglou, Shanqinglou, Xiqinglou, Gongqinglou, Fuqinglou, Huaqinglou and Fanqinglou. These are ten out of the forty-six Tulou listed as World Cultural Heritage sites. Most of them are well preserved, and still retain the original architectural structure making them rich in historical, architectural and artistic value. As such, Chuxi Tulou Cluster have become an important part of Fujian's representation on the World Cultural Heritage List.

◎ 土楼一隅。（王福平 摄）
A corner between Tulou. (Photo by Wang Fuping)

Chuxi Tulou Cluster is best known for having some of the most beautiful, the oldest, the most intact and the most famous Tulou. As a cluster, they are known for some unique characteristics such as the close proximity of the earthen buildings to each other. The people who live there also belong to one clan and thus there is one surname in the community. All of the buildings face one direction. These are only some of the special features. Due to Feng Shui and defence measure reasons, the earthen buildings only have one entrance at the north. An ever-flowing stream of water runs in front of the buildings reducing the need for wells within the earthen walls. For more than 600 years, most of the earthen buildings have been associated with the character "庆" (pronounced Qing). Perhaps it is because the Xu ancestors wanted their future generations to embrace the character's meanings: elegance, warmth and morality. The character "庆" also represents joy and auspiciousness, and the Xu ancestors may have hoped to hold on to these meanings through generation after generation, wishing their people the best and to be prosperous.

Chuxi Tulou Cluster exhibits the phenomenal combination of natural landscapes and historical villages. Within the depths of the steep mountains and complex terrain sits a spectacular village of earthen buildings, a perfect representation of harmony between man and nature.

The cluster is located in Chuxi Village which is listed as one of the "Chinese Traditional Villages" in November 2014. The village has stood witness to the ancient Hakka village's historical development that has preserved the original and natural features of Fujian Tulou.

◎ 初溪之夜。(李鸾汉 摄)
The night view of Chuxi Tulou Cluster. (Photo by Li Luanhan)

© 云水之间。（王福平 摄）
Between the clouds and water. (Photo by Wang Fuping)

◎ 集庆楼。(胡家新 摄)

Jiqinglou. (Photo by Hu Jiaxin)

■ 集庆楼

经过村中小溪，沿着石头路拾阶而上，右边最大的圆楼就是集庆楼。这座直径66米、高4层、占地2,826平方米的集庆楼堪称初溪土楼群的代表，由初溪村徐氏三世祖七兄弟建于1419年（明朝），距今已有600多年，为永定现存圆楼中年代最久远、结构最特殊的一座。

■ Jiqinglou

Stepping over the stone road in the village, the largest round building is on the right. This is Jiqinglou. The building stands 66 metres in diameter, has four storeys and covers an area of 2,826 square metres. An iconic representative of the cluster, it was built in 1419 of the Ming Dynasty by seven Xu brothers. Jiqinglou has stood for over 600 years and is the oldest and most unique circular structure in Yongding.

该楼底层墙厚1.6米，后人在墙外表用鹅卵石加砌1米多高的石墙裙，以防土墙被屋檐水溅湿。整座土楼所有房间、楼梯、隔墙全部用杉木材料构建，不用一枚铁钉，全靠榫卯结构衔接，不能不说是一个奇迹。建楼时集庆楼不像其他土楼设有几部楼梯，而是只在门厅东侧设置了一部楼梯。

后来在清朝乾隆年间维修该楼时，按底层每户从一楼到四楼各自安装楼梯，各层通道用薄薄的杉木板隔开，各户自成一个单元。在动荡年代里，既可以聚族而居，又可以彼此独立，不得不说是一种创新。如果本楼遇到外敌侵袭，就可以把这些杉木隔板打开，形成环楼内通廊，楼内的人一样可以在土楼里面灵活地进行防卫。该楼外环二层以上在每单元的梯间靠外墙处，都有一个外人无法发现的宽50厘米的暗梯，平时用木板盖住，遇到紧急情况时才使用。该楼后侧底层还设有一个秘密通道，在一个房间的外墙预留距地面约1.1米、高1.6米、宽1米的缺口，外面用与土墙相同的泥土封住，旧时用橱柜遮住，外人进入该房间亦无法发现其中奥秘。万一楼内居民需紧急疏散、外出避难时，可迅速捅开这个求生通道，直奔楼后的山坡，消失在树林之中。除了具备其他土楼用水或者沙子灭火的防卫设施以外，该楼外环第四层外墙外挑设有9个瞭望台，不仅可以观察楼外动静，还可在此架设土铳，凭险踞守。

集庆楼还有一个亮点。登上吱呀作响的古老木梯，步入博物馆，便可以看到旧时土楼居民用于生活、生产、娱乐的一些老物件，还有客家姓氏渊源展、土楼建筑艺术、客家民俗文物等，可以尽情探寻土楼客家人的生活密码，领略原汁原味的土楼文化积淀。

◎ 集庆楼内景。(陈军 摄)
Interior view of Jiqinglou. (Photo by Chen Jun)

The base of the building is 1.6 metres thick. Later generations would eventually use cobblestone to build a barrier that stands about one metre to encircle the earthen walls from being splashed by water. All the rooms, stairs and partitions of the building are constructed from fir wood. It does not need nails and is dependent on structure—some would say it was a bit of a miracle. Unlike the other buildings, when Jiqinglou was constructed, there were not multiple staircases put in place, instead there is only one staircase on the east side of the entrance hall.

It was not until later during the Qing Dynasty that renovations on the building resulted in more staircases being put in place from the first to the fourth floor. Each floor was separated by thin fir boards, and each household became a unit. This design is creative as the residents could live together while still having privacy.

Their innovation for protective measures is also admirable. Should there be an attack, the fir partitions could be opened to form an extended circular corridor inside the ring-shaped building. This provided the residents with the flexibility to move within the building as they defended themselves. Each unit has a ladder that reaches to the outer wall as well as a fifty-centimetre-wide ladder invisible to the eyes of an outsider. This ladder is usually covered with wooden boards and only used in cases of emergency. There are also secret passages on the lower level of the building. A gap exists between the outer wall and the rooms, about 1.1 metres off the ground, and 1.6 metres in height and 1 metre in width. It is sealed with the same soil that made the Tulou walls, and used to be covered by cabinets so that outsiders could not find it easily. In the case of an emergency evacuation, the residents can quickly access the survival route and go straight to the mountain side behind the buildings, making an escape into the woods. In addition to having fire extinguishing processes in place, the building has nine observation decks on the fourth floor outer ring. It not only allows direct sight of the movements outside the building, but also for someone to stand guard.

Another interest in Jiqinglou is the museum. Ascend the old creaky wooden ladders and walk into the museum, one can find traditional items used for living and entertainment. There is also a display of the Hakka family names, art originating from the Tulou and Hakka folk art objects that tell the guarded secrets of Hakka families. This is where the authentic Tulou culture has accumulated.

◎ 这里仿佛是一个梯的世界。72部楼梯把全楼分割成72个独立的单元。（王福平 摄）
A world of staircases. 72 staircases divide the building into 72 household units. (Photo by Wang Fuping)

■ 庚庆楼

紧挨着集庆楼的圆楼便是占地面积约660平方米的庚庆楼。这座建于清道光二十九年（1849）的圆楼，直径33米，正好是集庆楼的一半。庚庆楼高3层，共有111个房间。楼内有一层回廊屋，回廊屋里面一个天井，两个通道，其中一个通道正对着大门，另外一个通道连着大楼的侧门，方便来往于集庆楼。

庚庆楼木构件保存完好，至今仍有客家人居住。土楼里闲庭漫步的鸡鸭，四处悬挂的农具，几根晾衣竹竿，都让这个小世界充满浓浓的田园生活气息。

■ Gengqinglou

The round building next to Jiqinglou, known as Gengqinglou, was built in 1849 of the Qing Dynasty. It has an area of 660 square metres, and stretches 33 metres in diameter which is exactly half of Jiqinglou. Being three storeys high, there are 111 rooms in Gengqinglou. Within the walls of the building, there is a courtyard and two passageways next to the cloister. One of these leads to the main gate while the other connects to a side gate leading to Jiqinglou.

Gengqinglou is well preserved in terms of the wood work and thus, many Hakkas still live there. Poultry strut around in the courtyard and agricultural tools can be seen hung up. A few bamboo clothing poles scattered here and there make the small world within the walls a dynamic place to live.

◎ 庚庆楼。（赖永生 摄）
Gengqinglou. (Photo by Lai Yongsheng)

◎ 庚庆楼前玩耍的孩子。(胡家新 摄)
Children in front of the building. (Photo by Hu Jiaxin)

■ 余庆楼

在庚庆楼的东边是建于1729年的余庆楼，距今已有290多年历史，年代上仅次于集庆楼。该楼占地面积1,256平方米，高3层，每层34开间，设4部楼梯。从小路向余庆楼行走大约10多米，可以看见一个被石头封住的老大门，这是该楼初建时的楼门，原来楼名为东安楼，后因风水原因，便把楼门的朝向改为现在的方向，楼名也更改为余庆楼。

余庆楼门坪不大，下方是深约20多米的山谷，山谷下面就是村里的小溪。如今的余庆楼已被后人改设为民宿，夜深人静的时候，入住这座历经两百多年的土楼，聆听窗外潺潺的流水声，鸡犬相闻，恍若隔世。

◎ 夕阳下的余庆楼。（胡家新 摄）
Yuqinglou at sunset. (Photo by Hu Jiaxin)

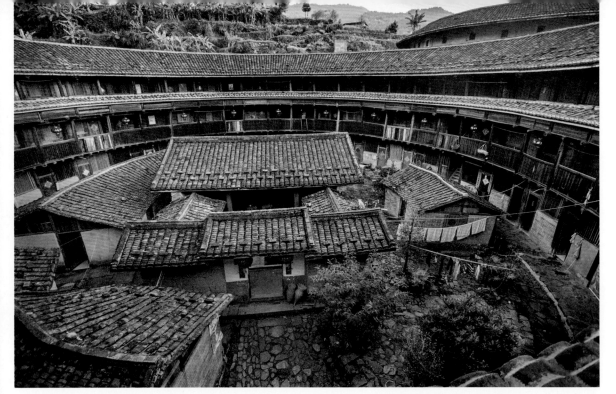

◎ 余庆楼内景。（胡家新 摄）

The interior sight of Yuqinglou. (Photo by Hu Jiaxin)

■ Yuqinglou

To the east of Gengqinglou is Yuqinglou. Built in 1729, its history stretches about 290 years and is second only to Jiqinglou. The building covers an area of 1,256 square metres and is 3 storeys high. Each floor has 34 rooms and 4 staircases. About ten metres along the path towards Yuqinglou, a closed stone gate can be seen. This was the original main entrance when the Tulou was built and was named Dong'anlou. However, due to Feng Shui reasons, the orientation of the building entrance was changed to its current direction and the building's name was changed to Yuqinglou.

Outside the main entrance of Yuqinglou is a valley about twenty-metres deep with a creek that flows into the village. Today, Yuqinglou has been converted into accommodation by the descendants. On a quiet night, staying in the two-hundred-year-old earth building allows you to hear the sounds of the running water outside the window, and the dogs can be heard communicating with one another from separate directions.

■ 绳庆楼

　　"三圆一方"土楼中紧挨着集庆楼的唯一一座方楼就是绳庆楼。该楼建于1799年，占地面积1,482平方米，由一座正方形土楼和一个方形回廊屋组合而成，回廊屋里还有一个围合而成的厅堂，其形很像一个"回"字。外楼宽39米，深27米，高4层，只有1个大门；全楼168个房间、2个厅堂，设4部楼梯。

　　据说，绳庆楼居民的先祖们在外围四层土楼与厅堂之间留有很大的天井，供子孙们在此修建了一层回廊屋和一个精美的厅堂，成为初溪土楼群里唯一一座"方中套方"的方形土楼。

◎ 回字形的绳庆楼。（胡家新 摄）
In the shape of the Chinese character"回". (Photo by Hu Jiaxin)

■ Shengqinglou

Shengqinglou is square and was built in 1799. The building covers an area of 1,482 square metres and is composed of a square earthen building and a square cloister house. There is also an enclosed hall inside the cloister house, making the whole layout look like the Chinese character "回" which means to return. The outer building is 39 metres wide, 27 metres deep and 4 storeys high with only one main entrance. The entire building itself has 168 rooms, 2 halls and 4 staircases.

It is said that the ancestors of Shengqing building had a large patio between the four walls and the hall, where the children and grandchildren built a cloister house and a beautiful hall, making Shengqinglou the only one like it out of Chuxi Tulou Cluster.

◎ 方中套方。（胡家新 摄）
A square building inside the outer square Tulou. (Photo by Hu Jiaxin)

■ 善庆楼

　　村子里格外抢眼的唯一一座白楼是建于1978年的善庆楼，是最年轻的土楼，为华侨捐资修建的徐氏民居。土楼占地1,200平方米，土木结构，高3层，每层26开间。大门旁嵌有一石碑，上面刻有"善庆楼志"，记载了建设该楼的出资人，并希望子孙后代感恩祖先之恩德。这是福建"世遗"土楼中唯一一座刻有楼志的土楼。

　　善庆楼最独特的建筑特色是一楼门厅、走廊及天井全部由同一规格的方形花岗岩铺就，外墙以石灰粉刷，通风透光性能极佳，别具一格。该楼是中国生土夯筑技术得到良好传承的实物例证。

◎ 善庆楼窗外悬挂的空调张扬着其年轻的身份。（胡家新 摄）
The air conditioners hanging outside the windows of Shanqinglou exhibits its updates with modernity. (Photo by Hu Jiaxin)

◎ 花岗岩铺就的内院。（胡家新 摄）
The granite-paved courtyard. (Photo by Hu Jiaxin)

■ Shanqinglou

Known as the only white building in the village, Shanginglou was built in 1978 and is the youngest out of the cluster. The members of the Xu clan had built it with the donations from those who have immigrated overseas. It covers an area of 1,200 square metres, with a wooden structure and three floors, each of which has 26 rooms. There is also a stone monument inscribed next to the gate of the building. Upon it is engraved "Shanqinglou" and records the funders who built the building along with their hopes that the future generations will be grateful for the ancestors' kindness. This is the only monument appearing on Fujian Tulou.

There are three unique architectural features of Shanqinglou. First is that its foyer, the corridor and courtyard are paved with square granite of the same specifications. The second is that the exterior walls are painted with lime and thirdly, the Tulou has excellent ventilation and light transmission properties. This building is a real example of the tamping technique for earth buildings.

■ 锡庆楼

　　锡庆楼坐落于初溪村中部，是一座建于1849年的长方形土楼，占地面积700余平方米。三个楼层中，第一层有20个房间和两个厅，二、三层各23个房间。楼内有两部楼梯、大小两个门。锡庆楼的旁边是一条穿越初溪村的小溪。旧时，附近几座土楼都在这条小溪挑水饮用，因此建有侧门，出门便是小溪，方便了取水。

■ Xiqinglou

Xiqinglou is located in the middle of Chuxi Village. It is a rectangular earthen building built in 1849, covering an area of more than 700 square metres. Among the three floors, there are 20 rooms and two halls on the first floor, and 23 rooms on the second and third floors. There are two staircases and two doors in the building.

Next to Xiqinglou is a small stream that crosses the village of Chuxi. In the old days, this served a source of drinking water for many of the nearby Tulou. As a result, there is a side door on the left-hand side which facilitates access to the small stream.

◎ 长方形的锡庆楼。（胡家新 摄）
The rectangular building Xiqinglou. (Photo by Hu Jiaxin)

◎ 六角形的共庆楼。（胡家新 摄）
The hexagonal building Gongqinglou. (Photo by Hu Jiaxin)

■ 共庆楼

在列入世界文化遗产的土楼中，共庆楼是唯一一座六角形土楼，建于1949年，坐落于初溪村东部，占地面积约3,500平方米，是一座面阔40米、进深31米的4层土楼。整座土楼设4部楼梯、1个大门，有152个房间（厅）。建楼时因为地处梯田，所以地形前低后高，里面的建筑高低层次错落有致，采光显得更好。又因墙角对着祠堂，据说是为了避免破坏风水，于是将前面的两个墙角削平，所以便成为现在的六角楼。

■ Gongqinglou

Out of all the Tulou listed on the World Heritage List, Gongqinglou is the only hexagonal Tulou. It was built in 1949 and is located in the east of Chuxi Village. Covering an area of about 3,500 square metres, it has four storeys, a width of 40 metres and a depth of 31 metres. There are four staircases, one main entrance gate and 152 rooms.

The building was built on terraced fields so the interior has followed nature's structure. The high-low concept allows for better lighting within the Tulou. In order to avoid the Feng Shui problem, the front two corners were flattened to make it the current hexagonal shape building we see today.

◎ 椭圆形的福庆楼。（胡家新 摄）

The oval shape building Fuqinglou. (Photo by Hu Jiaxin)

■ 福庆楼

福庆楼占地面积660平方米，也是一座比较小型的土楼。该楼建于1849年，3层高，每层有30个房间，设有1个厅、3部楼梯和1个大门。楼内也有一排回廊屋和一个围合而成的厅堂，没有后厅。

跟其他土楼不一样的是，福庆楼是一座椭圆形土楼，因建楼时受地方所限，两边土墙往楼内缩进一点，于是本来圆形的土楼就变成了接近椭圆形。楼内虽小，却处处可见楼主人常用的生活用具；坐在木板凳上的老人、四处忙碌着的主人，让人感到亲切而温馨，依稀看到土楼人家的朝朝暮暮。

■ Fuqinglou

Fuqinglou covers an area of 660 square metres and is a relatively small Tulou. The building was built in 1849 and is three storeys high. There are 30 rooms on each floor, with one hall, three staircases and one main entrance gate. There are also a row of porch houses and an enclosed hall in the building. Unlike the other Tulou, Fuqinglou is elliptical in shape. Because of the limited space when the Tulou was constructed, the two outer earth walls are closer to the inner walls, giving it the oval shape that it is. Although the building is small, the everyday objects used by the residents are everywhere. The elderly sitting on their wooden benches and the bustling residents going about their daily tasks bring warmth to those who are lucky enough to see it.

■ 华庆楼

华庆楼建于清道光年间的1829年，是一座占地约480平方米的长方形土楼，高2层，有前厅和后厅，中间1个天井，全楼设2部楼梯，1个大门。

华庆楼是初溪土楼群最小的"世遗"土楼，如今还有一户徐姓后人在里面居住。这座土楼面积较小，但这个家族的人在里面已生活了将近200年，楼里挂着一些简单的生活用具，可以想象出楼主人原生态的生活场景。

■ Huaqinglou

Huaqinglou was built in 1829 of the Qing Dynasty. It is a rectangular Tulou that covers 480 square metres in area and is two storeys high. There are front and back halls with a courtyard in the middle. This Tulou has two staircases and one main entrance gate.

Huanqinglou is the smallest Tulou out of those listed by UNESCO. Today, there are Xu descendants who live in the building. Although small in size, the family have lived in it for nearly 200 years. From the simple items used within this Tulou, one can imagine the harmony which the people live in.

◎ 初溪土楼群里最小的土楼。（胡家新 摄）
The smallest Tulou in the cluster. (Photo by Hu Jiaxin)

■ 藩庆楼

坐落于初溪村中部、集庆楼南侧的藩庆楼建于1949年，高4层，全楼设4部楼梯，1个大门，是一座长方形的土楼，土楼中间设有厅堂，是一座比较有现代建筑特色的土楼。

国家级非物质文化遗产项目——客家土楼营造技艺的代表性传承人徐松生出生在余庆楼，他6岁时跟随家人搬进藩庆楼，在该楼住了将近20年，对童年的土楼生活历历在目。凭着对土楼的深厚感情，他高中毕业以后跟随父亲学习泥水木作等土楼建筑技术，在其父亲的言传身教下，加上他勤学苦练和善于摸索，他的建筑技术有了突飞猛进的提高。2001年，年久失修、面临倒塌危险的集庆楼、余庆楼在他的精心维修下，恢复了原貌。

◎ 藩庆楼。（胡家新 摄）
Fanqinglou. (Photo by Hu Jiaxin)

◎ 藩庆楼俯视图。（胡家新 摄）
An aerial view of Fanqinglou. (Photo by Hu Jiaxin)

▌ Fanqinglou

Located in the middle of Chuxi Village, and to the south of Jiqinglou, Fanqinglou was built in 1949. It is four storeys high, has four staircases and one main entrance gate. It is a rectangular Tulou with a hall situated in the middle. It is considered to have more modern features compared to other Tulou.

Xu Songsheng, a representative inheritor of the Hakka Tulou building skills, a National Intangible Cultural Heritage Project, was born in Yuqinglou. At the age of 6, he moved to Fanqinglou with his family where he has continued to live for almost 20 years, leaving him with deep memories of the Tulou. After finishing high school, Xu followed his father to study Tulou building techniques, motivated by his strong sense of familiarity to his childhood home. Under his father's guidance, coupled with his hard work and own exploration, Xu's building technique has improved leaps and bounds. In 2001, Jiqinglou and Yuqinglou seriously needed repairs and faced the danger of collapsing. It was under his meticulous eye that the buildings recovered their original appearance after maintenance.

永定洪坑土楼群

　　洪坑土楼群位于永定区东南面的湖坑镇洪坑村，距永定城区45千米。洪坑土楼群由林氏祖先始建于13世纪，保存完好的有数十座16世纪以来修建的土楼，大小交错，形态各异，主要有正方形、长方形、圆形、五凤楼、半月形及其变异形式的土楼造型。其中7座被列入《世界遗产名录》，包括振成楼、庆成楼、福裕楼、福兴楼、如升楼、光裕楼和奎聚楼。

　　洪坑村三面环山，林木葱茏。一条小溪自北而南蜿蜒曲折，贯穿全村。一座座风格不一、年代不同的土楼沿溪而建、依山傍水。村口的老水车像时钟一样转动着。小桥、流水、水车、田园和土楼，与耸立的群山、漂浮的白云，构成一幅自然古朴、和谐美丽的宁静画卷。

◎ 永定洪坑土楼群。（胡家新 摄）
Hongkeng Tulou Cluster in Yongding. (Photo by Hu Jiaxin)

Hongkeng Tulou Cluster in Yongding

Hongkeng Tulou Cluster is located in Hongkeng Village of Hukeng Town which is in the southeastern part of Yongding District. It is 45 kilometres away from the downtown. The cluster was started in the 13th century by the Lin's ancestors, leaving dozens of Tulou well-preserved which had been built since the 16th century of the Ming Dynasty. The cluster mainly consists of square, rectangular and circular Tulou, half-moon shape and five-phoenix-style (pavilion) buildings. There are seven Tulou of the cluster listed as the World Heritage sites.

Hongkeng Village is surrounded by mountains on three sides and has lush forests. A small stream weaves and bends from north to south, running through the village. The Tulou built along the stream are of different styles and ages. There is an old waterwheel at the entrance of the village which continuously turns. Small bridges, flowing water, windmills, fields and Tulou amongst towering mountains and floating white clouds form a picturesque display of nature's simplicity, harmony and beauty.

◎ 夜雨中已闭门的院落。（冯木波 摄）
Separated units on a rainy night. (Photo by Feng Mubo)

■ 振成楼

以富丽堂皇、内部空间设计精致多变而著称的振成楼是洪坑土楼群的代表，也是客家土楼中按照八卦图设计，淋漓尽致展现中华传统文化的典型代表。振成楼建于1912年，占地面积约5,000平方米，高4层，直径57.2米。楼内按《易经》八卦原理布局，以青砖防火墙将圆楼分隔成8个辐射状的等分。每卦关起门户，自成院落；打开门户，全楼贯通。该楼每层两个厅和44个房间，内外三环共有208个房间。底层每单元各自与内环天井围合成一个院落。

■ Zhenchenglou

Zhenchenglou is famous for its splendid design and exquisite interiors. It is the most well-known Tulou out of the Hongkeng Tulou Cluster. It embodies China's traditional culture. The earthen building was built in 1912 and covers an area of about 5,000 square metres. It is four storeys high and spans 57.2 metres in diameter. The building is laid out according to the traditional Chinese Bagua diagram–the eight trigrams of *The Book of Changes*. Brick firewalls separate eight equal units to represent the eight diagrams. There are two halls and forty-four rooms on each floor of the building, totaling 208 rooms. Each unit on the lower floor is connected to the inner ring patio to form a courtyard.

楼内特别引人注目的是位于该楼内环的厅堂，其中心大厅有两层楼高，立有4根直径约0.7米、高近7米的具有西方风格的圆形花岗石柱，擎起长9米、宽约40厘米的石梁。大厅高大宽敞，不仅有其他土楼厅堂的功能，还可作为一个独具特色的演戏台。

振成楼的内部装饰工艺精巧、图案精美典雅，具有深厚的文化底蕴。楼内门厅等处悬挂名人的题词、题诗，处处可见爱国爱家、勤俭廉洁、积德行善的楹联，让人深深感受到这座土楼里传承弘扬爱国奋斗精神和中华优秀传统文化的浓厚氛围。

What is particularly striking in the building is the hall behind the inner ring. The central hall is two storeys high and sits above the inner ring roof. In front of the platforms, there are four circular granite columns with a diameter of nearly 0.7 metre, and a height close to 7 metres. supporting a stone beam with a length of 9 metres and as thick as 0.4 metre. The difference between this hall and other Tulou halls is that it can serve as a stage.

The interior decoration of Zhenchenglou is simple yet elegant with profound cultural heritage. The inscriptions and poems of celebrities are hung in the foyer of the building. There is a strong atmosphere of patriotism and integrity which reflects the Chinese traditional culture.

◎ 精致多变的内部设计。（李艺爽 摄）
Exquisite interiors. (Photo by Li Yishuang)

振成楼的主体是圆楼，左右两边是对称的半月形厢房，远远看去犹如一项旧官帽，楼前面的洪川溪好像是古代官服上面的佩带，楼的后面跟几座大山像是一把椅子、一个案台和两个扶手。整体想象，似乎有一名官员坐在太师椅上办案。

The general structure of Zhenchenglou is circular with the left and right sides made up of symmetrical half-moon shaped rooms, looking like an old Chinese official's hat from afar. The Hongchuan Stream that flows in front of the Tulou is likened to an accessory on a traditional official's uniform while the back of the building alongside the mountains mimics a chair, a desk and two handrails. Some would say that from certain angles, it would seem like an official sitting on the chair of the Grand Master.

◎ 宛如椅子上办案的古代官员。（陈军 摄）
　Looking like an official sitting in a chair. (Photo by Chen Jun)

◎ 被誉为"土楼王子"的建筑杰作。（张耀辉 摄）
A masterpiece known as the "Prince of Tulou". (Photo by Zhang Yaohui)

振成楼内独特的中西合璧建筑风格以及大胆采用的色调，充分体现了西方建筑美学所强调的多样统一原则，开创了将西方建筑文化融入客家土楼建筑的先河，不仅极具美感，还具有很高的研究价值，堪称杰作，不愧是"建筑奇葩""土楼王子"。1986年4月，在美国洛杉矶，振成楼模型和雍和宫、长城的模型一同出现在世界建筑模型展览会上，引起世人瞩目，轰动一时。

The unique architecture and bold colours of Zhenchenglou reflect the use of diverse Chinese and Western aesthetics. It has created a precedent for integrating Western architectural influences into the Hakka Tulou. Not only is it beautiful to see but has high research value. Zhenchenglou stands as a masterpiece worthy to be known as the "Prince of Tulou Architecture" within China. In April 1986, models of Zhenchenglou, Lama Yonghe Temple and the Great Wall were exhibited at the World Architecture Model Exhibition in Los Angeles where they attracted worldwide attention.

■ 庆成楼

庆成楼坐落在洪坑村东部，从振成楼大门出来往左边不远处，便可以见到这座建于民国二十六年（1937年）的正方形土楼。该楼坐东北朝西南，占地面积约1,100平方米，高3层，4部楼梯，1个大门，1口水井，后厅为厅堂。

2014年6月，全国首家"客家家训馆"在庆成楼开馆。展厅按客家源流、家训家规、客家厅堂、楹联匾额、家训故事、客家私塾、客家俗语、家庭美德、资料查阅电子屏、客家家训馆宣传折页10个部分进行展陈。集中展示了土楼客家人的祖训家规，充分体现了客家土楼的文化内涵。

在庆成楼的天井里，有几张长椅子供游客休息，椅子旁边的墙上有一个特制的"𠊎"字，这是客家话"我"的意思。这个千百年来烙印在客家人灵魂里的"𠊎"字，维系着分布在世界各地的客家人的原乡情怀。

◎ 庆成楼。（胡家新 摄）
Qingchenglou. (Photo by Hu Jiaxin)

◎ 庆成楼内景。（胡家新 摄）
Interior sight of Qingchenglou. (Photo by Hu Jiaxin)

■ Qingchenglou

Qingchenglou is located in the eastern part of Hongkeng Village. Turn left after walking out of Zhenchenglou and one can see this square building. Built in 1937, it covers an area of about 1,110 square metres, has three storeys, four staircases, one gate, one well, and a back hall.

In June 2014, the first Hakka Family Education Hall was opened in Qingchenglou. The exhibition hall is split into ten different display sections: the origins of the Hakka community, Hakka virtues, Hakka traditions within the home, Hakka hall layouts, plaques, age-old folk stories, Hakka idioms, a modern information area, schooling within the Hakka community and common door couplets. The exhibition full of ancestral traditions of the Hakka Tulou and people reflects the strong cultural value the earthen buildings hold in Chinese culture.

In the courtyard of Qingchenglou, there are several benches for tourists to rest on. There is a special character placed on the wall next to the chairs which means "I" in the Hakka dialect. This character has come to be a brand that has imprinted in the memories for the Hakka people for thousands of years. No matter where the Hakka people are around the world, it gives them a sense of identity.

◎ 人在画中。（胡家新 摄）

Living on a picturesque land. (Photo by Hu Jiaxin)

■ 福裕楼

　　沿着振成楼门前的小溪往上走不远，便来到福裕楼的观景台。福裕楼背靠青山，楼前有三个大门，门前是一块用当地鹅卵石铺砌的长方形门坪，门坪前面用砖块砌成约2.3米高的围墙，其他各段围墙则用鹅卵石砌成。门前清澈的小溪旁长着青绿色的芭蕉叶和竹叶，四周鹅卵石铺成的小路弯弯曲曲，这些与福裕楼淡黄的外墙衬托在一起，好一幅青山绿水画面。

　　福裕楼建于1880年，占地面积约4,000平方米，属于四进三落府第式（五凤楼）。福裕楼秀外慧中、富丽堂皇、气宇不凡，堪称永定府第式土楼的杰出代表、五凤楼的经典。

■ Fuyulou

Walking up along the stream in front Zhenchenglou, one can see the observation deck of Fuyulou where you can see Fuyulou standing against a green mountain. Fuyulou has three main gates but before reaching these, there is a rectangular doorway made of locally sourced cobblestones which then extends to a wall that rises 2.3 metres high. All the other walls are also made of cobblestones. There is a stream that flows in front of the doorway and beside it grows green banana leaves and bamboo leaves that line the cobblestoned roads. Together, this creates a simple yet stunning picture of greenery, mountain scenery and trickling water.

Fuyulou was built in 1880 and covers an area of about 4,000 square metres. Although not as popular as the circular and rectangular shaped Tulou, it is categorised as the third type, the five-phoenix-style building and a classic representation of its kind.

走进福裕楼内，便可看见几扇年代久远的中门和天井。楼内装饰非常讲究，处处透着中式的古典美。有形态逼真的石雕、造型优美的木雕，有古色古香的几案供桌，有惟妙惟肖的泥塑，有绚丽多姿、至今色彩明艳的彩塑作品。楼内到处可见的书画精湛不俗，均出自书法名家之手。

◎ 精致的装饰。（胡家新 摄）
Elaborate decorations. (Photo by Hu Jiaxin)

Walking into Fuyulou, immediately one can see some quaint doors and the courtyard. The interior is particular with beautiful classical Chinese designs. There are realistic stone carvings, sleek wood carvings, antique furniture pieces and vivid clay sculptures. Paintings and calligraphy works can be seen hanging everywhere, showing the splendid talents of calligraphy masters.

◎ 华灯初上。（陈军 摄）
When the lights on. (Photo by Chen Jun)

◎ 月光如洗。（冯木波 摄）

Painted with moonlights. (Photo by Feng Mubo)

　　福裕楼前楼高2层，后楼高5层半，两侧高5层。楼后堂比中堂高一个台阶，中堂比前堂高两个台阶，前后楼高低有序，主次分明，强调纵横之间的对称，高低中又有些许变化。后堂底层为厨房、餐厅、客厅，二层为粮仓，三层以上为卧室。前、中、后楼屋顶由前往后层层升高，因此屋顶坡度比其他类型土楼的大很多。楼内共有166个房间、22个厅堂、28部楼梯、2个侧门、2口水井。6个天井使楼内内部空间层次更为分明。下雨天的时候，慢悠悠地走在天井旁边的走廊上，一边感受着土楼的古朴和神奇，一边观看雨水从四角天空飘落，何尝不是一种享受呢？

The front part of the building is two storeys high while the back rises five and a half storeys high and side components five storeys high. All parts are of vertical and horizontal symmetry. Each segment is elevated more than the segment before it in a terrace like manner. At the lowest level of the back component you can find the kitchen, dining room and living room. On the second floor is the granary while bedrooms can be found on the third floor. As the building stacks higher, the slope of the roofs is steeper than most other types of Tulou. In total, there are 166 rooms, 22 halls, 28 staircases, two side doors and six patios, and two wells. On a rainy day, as you walk slowly down the corridor next to the patio, you will feel a strong appreciation for the simplicity and magic of the Tulou. There is nothing more pleasing than watching the raindrops fall from the sky and run down the eaves.

■ 福兴楼

福兴楼位于振成楼西北侧，是建于清道光年间（1821—1850）的一座长方形土楼，占地面积约800平方米，高3层，设4部楼梯，1口水井。这座历经100多年风雨的土楼，里面依然住着几户人家。虽然简单朴素，很难看见绚丽多彩的装饰，但能让人真真切切地感受到土楼人家自给自足的田园生活。土楼里面的每一块木板，每一面斑驳的土墙，都能看到岁月的痕迹，让人想象她的过往。

■ Fuxinglou

Fuxinglou is located to the northwest of Zhenchenglou. It is a rectangular Tulou built during 1821—1850 of the Qing Dynasty. It covers an area of 800 square metres, has three storeys, four staircases and a well. Although Fuxinglou has experienced over a hundred years of history, it is rather simple and still home for several families. It is hard to find colourful décor here but, there are many farmer's tools and several household appliances suggesting the self-sufficient and idyllic life within the walls. Every piece of wood used and every mottled wall in this Tulou have been imprinted with traces of history, allowing visitors to imagine the vicissitudes that may have occurred in the past.

◎ 金色阳光洒满福兴楼。（赖永生 摄）
Fuxinglou under the sun. (Photo by Lai Yongsheng)

◎ 简朴狭窄的空间。（赖永生 摄）
The simple and narrow inside. (Photo by Lai Yongsheng)

■ 如升楼

如升楼在福裕楼的斜对面，小小的如升楼看上去很像旧时客家人用竹筒制作的量米工具（俗称"米升"），所以当地人常称之为"米升楼"，也有游客称之为"袖珍土楼"，是福建"世遗"土楼中最小的土楼。国产动漫大片《大鱼海棠》中灵婆所在的如升楼即以此楼为原型。

如升楼建于清光绪年间（1875—1908），坐东朝西，占地面积约为500平方米，高3层，直径23米。楼内空间极小，仅有几户人家，但是整座土楼看起来却井然有序。楼周边环境优美，楼前一条小石头路，通向清澈见底的洪川溪，小溪上架着一座石桥，承载着土楼人家的梦想。

■ Rushenglou

Rushenglou is diagonally opposite Fuyulou, and its small size looks a bit like the traditional bamboo tool the Hakka people used to measure rice. Rushenglou has been nicknamed by some tourists as the "Pocket Tulou" due to it being the smallest earthen building out of the listed World Heritage sites. In the Chinese made animation, *Big Fish and Begonia,* a character Lingpo lives in a Tulou, which is based off Rushenglou.

Rushenglou was built during 1875—1908 of the Qing Dynasty . Sitting in the east and facing west, it covers an area of about 500 square metres, has three floors, and is 23 metres in diameter. The space inside the building is very small and only a few families live there. As a result, the Tulou is very orderly. Rushenglou's surroundings are very quaint, with a small stone path at the front of the building connecting the clear Hongchuan Stream. A stone bridge allows for passage over the stream, which bears the locals' dream.

○ 小小的如升楼。（王福平 摄）
The Small "Pocket Tulou". (Photo by Wang Fuping)

■ 光裕楼

长方形的光裕楼，建于清乾隆四十年（1775），是洪坑土楼群历史最早、保留最完整的长方形土楼。它占地面积约2,500平方米，高3层，每层35个房间，设4部楼梯，1个大门，后厅为厅堂。因林氏先祖重视教育，光裕楼人才辈出，功名显赫。出过9位大夫、4位进士、40余位秀才，因此当地人又称该楼为"大夫第"。

从光裕楼的大门进去是一个很大的院落，这里经常举办婚庆民俗表演，所以在光裕楼的大门上挂着大红花，门口放着花轿等演出物品。进入光裕楼的大门，便可以看见内院有一个写有"大夫第"三个字的一层建筑，从内院进去走过两个小天井是大楼的后厅。楼内古色古香的装饰，依稀可看出昔日的辉煌和粗犷古朴的气势。土楼内外张灯结彩，人丁兴旺，让这座古老的土楼显得那么喜庆、那么生机勃勃。

◎ 人才辈出的古老光裕楼。（胡家新 摄）
The old Tulou with generations of talented residents. (Photo by Hu Jiaxin)

◎ 错落有致的屋顶。（胡家新 摄）
Amazing roofs of the building. (Photo by Hu Jiaxin)

■ Guangyulou

The rectangular Guangyulou was built in 1775, having seen the most throughout history and is the most intact rectangular Tulou in the Hongkeng Tulou Cluster. Covering about 2,500 square metres, it is three storeys high, and has 35 rooms on each floor and four staircases. There is one main entrance gate, and a back hall. Because the Lin ancestors of Guangyulou valued education, there have been generations of talented residents. Thirteen young men from Guangyulou became senior officials and over forty passed the imperial examination at the county level, hence the name "Dafudi" which references the talent that can be procured from Guangyulou.

Walking through the gate into Guangyulou, there is a large courtyard. There are often wedding celebrations show here so one will see many large red flowers hanging on the walls while props such as the wedding sedan chair are placed near the gate. Then passing the main gate, there is a sign saying "Dafudi" on the building as you head on through the inner courtyard. From there, one will pass two small patios as you head towards the back hall. The antique décor in the building provides a glimpse into the past of the rugged yet simple personality of Guangyulou. The lights inside and outside the Tulou are as bright as the thriving people within the walls, making the atmosphere vibrant and festive.

◎ 别具一格的宫殿式土楼。（赖永生 摄）

The unique palatial Tulou. (Photo by Lai Yongsheng)

■ **奎聚楼**

从福裕楼边门出来，不远处就是奎聚楼。奎聚楼始建于1834年，占地面积约6,000平方米，用了近5年时间建成，是一座比振成楼历史更早、面积更大的宫殿式结构的方形土楼，其建筑风格在福建土楼中也是别具一格的。

进入楼内，依次为大门、前厅、天井、中厅、天井、正厅，两侧为横楼，是一座呈左右对称的宫殿式建筑。内院套一个由主厅的前厅与中堂两边的回廊组成的一个小四合院。楼内有很多木结构建筑，檐梁雕刻十分精美，有的墙壁和屋脊上还有形式多样的绘画以及内容丰富的彩塑。后楼第二层至第四层的腰檐中段突出一段小屋顶，其中第二层突出的形成戏台，第三层、第四层前突幅度向上依次收缩，使正厅前向成四层屋檐，形成重重叠叠的建筑形体，远观颇有西藏布达拉宫的风格。

奎聚楼内东、西两边天井各有一口水井，当地人叫日月阴阳井，一深一浅。清澈的那口水井也称为"百年古井虎豹泉"，井水特别清洌甘甜，用这口井的水泡茶，味道独具特色。

从远处望去，整座楼与背后的山脊连成一体，山脉远而悠长、近而雄劲，犹如猛虎下山。奎聚楼即是"虎头"，大门旁边的墙上白白的石灰像是老虎的白额，大院的围墙中间正对大门处的两扇窗像是一对炯炯有神的虎眼，楼前田野上有两条自然隆起的地段，好像老虎的一双"前腿"。

■ Kuijulou

Stepping out from the side door of Fuyulou, one sees Kuijulou nearby. Built in 1834, Kuijulou covers an area of about 6,000 square metres and took nearly five years to construct. It is a palatial square-shaped earthen building that is even older and larger than Zhenchenglou. Its architectural style is also unique amongst the Fujian Tulou.

As you enter through Kuijulou's outer gate, you have the typical main entrance, front hall, patio, middle hall, patio and main hall layout. This creates a symmetrical palace-like design. The inner courtyard is composed of a porch in the main hall and a cloister on both sides of the middle hall. There are many wooden structures in the building, and the carvings on the beams are wonderfully artistic. Some walls and ridges have been painted with rich colours. Between the second and fourth floors of Kuijulou protrudes roof eaves. This creates a mini stage at the second level while the third and fourth slant above one another. As a result, the main hall has overlapping eaves going towards the centre. This design hints at architectural style of the Potala Palace in Tibet.

Wells can be located at the east and west sides of Kuijulou. The locals call them the Yin-Yang Wells, one of them is shallow and the other deep. One of the wells is known for its clear and sweet water. It is often used to brew tea, giving each cup a unique taste.

Looking at the building from afar, the way the Tulou sits against the mountainous backdrop emanates strength. Those with abstract minds could argue that it is a vision of a tiger coming down the mountains. Kuijulou is the tiger's head and the white walls extending from the gate are the white stripes on its head. Facing the gate in the courtyard are two windows that are like a pair of sacred tiger eyes while the two natural ridges at the front of the Tulou are a pair of front legs.

◎ 宫殿式设计。（冯木波 摄）
The palace-like design. (Photo by Feng Mupo)

永定高北土楼群

　　高北土楼群位于永定区东南面的高头乡高北村，距离永定城区47千米，土楼群后面是林木葱茏的青山，前面是一条自西而东缓缓流过的高头溪，溪两旁是高高耸立的大山、错落有致的土楼群以及宽阔的农田。在数十座规模不等、造型各异的土楼中，承启楼、世泽楼、五云楼、侨福楼四座土楼被列入《世界遗产名录》。这四座土楼由青石板小路连在一起，尤其是圆楼承启楼和方楼世泽楼因为紧相毗邻，形成一线天的奇观，方圆结合，相映成趣。

◎ 永定高北土楼群。（胡家新 摄）
Gaobei Tulou Cluster in Yongding. (Photo by Hu Jiaxin)

Gaobei Tulou Cluster in Yongding

Gaobei Tulou Cluster is located in Gaobei Village, Gaotou Township which is southeast of Yongding District. It is 47 kilometres away from the downtown. Behind the cluster are lush forests and at the front runs a stream flowing from west to east. On both sides of the stream are towering mountains, while a patchwork of Tulou and farmlands are scattered between. Among the many various shaped Tulou, four buildings are inscribed on the World Heritage List: Chengqilou, Wuyunlou, Shizelou and Qiaofulou. The four Tulou are connected by bluestone paths. The circular Chengqilou and rectangular Shizelou are adjacent to each other, creating a special sight of geometrical buildings and a unique view of "A Sliver of Sky" between the two roofs.

■ 承启楼

承启楼坐落在高北土楼群的中心位置，始建于明崇祯年间（1628—1644），之后经历三代人，依次建造第二环、第三环和第四环，清康熙四十八年（1709）落成，历时半个世纪。全楼由四环构成，环与环之间以鹅卵石砌筑的天井相隔，以石砌廊道或小道相连。全楼按《易经》八卦进行布局。中堂表示太极，太极生两仪，将中堂一分为二；外环主楼用四道土墙把楼平均分成了四大块，表示两仪生四象；每象中间都设有一部楼梯，把楼分成了八个卦；每卦又有八个卧室，达到八八六十四个房间即六十四卦。这种根据天体运动和自然规律的八卦布局，把天、地、人、楼自然地融为一体，达到了土楼民居建筑的最高境界。纵观承启楼的整个布局、庞大的建筑以及久远的年代，真可谓是"高四层，楼四圈，上上下下四百间；圆中圆，圈套圈，历经沧桑三百年"。

◎ 土楼之王承启楼。（胡家新 摄）
The king of the Tulou. (Photo by Hu Jiaxin)

◎ 承启楼内景。（胡家新 摄）

The interiors of Chengqilou. (Photo by Hu Jiaxin)

■ Chengqilou

Chengqilou is located in the centre of Gaobei Tulou Cluster. Construction started in the Ming Dynasty between 1628—1644 and lasted around half a century. Throughout the next three generations, the second, third and fourth rings were built in turn before being completed in 1709 of the Qing Dynasty. Chengqilou is composed of four rings, which are separated by cobblestone built patios and connected by stone corridors or paths. The layout of this Tulou is in accordance to Bagua following the movements of the celestial bodies and natural laws that integrate heaven, earth, people and buildings so that the Feng Shui requirements can be met.

◎ 夜火阑珊。（王福平 摄）

While the lights on. (Photo by Wang Fuping)

承启楼外环（即主楼）直径为72米，高4层14米，每层64个房间。东、西面各有两部楼梯，正面(南面)开一大门，东西两侧各开一个侧门。第二环由36个房间组成，其中西侧有6个房间为两层，其余为单层。第二环除正面和东、西两侧各以一个开间作为通道外，其余各间与前向的小庭院、青砖隔墙围合成小院落，每个院落各开一门，与三环后侧的内通廊相通。第三环是一个由20个房间组成的单层，旧时楼主崇文重教，为了使楼内的女孩子既能够知书达理，又不跟外面的男孩子一起读书，便在此开办了私塾。第四环是主厅，是一个占地30多平方米的单层，处于全楼的核心位置，是整个家族最高权力的象征。厅堂后上方、前向屋檐下以及两侧的木柱上，悬挂着清代以来名人赠送的题匾和楹联。

承启楼占地面积5,300多平方米，全楼外高内低，逐环递减。它具有高大厚重、粗犷雄伟的建筑风格，悠久的历史以及独特的造型，堪称永定土楼中规模最大、环数最多的圆形土楼，享有"土楼王"的美誉，被收入无数书刊。1986年，承启楼作为"福建民居"的图案印在我国发行的中国民居邮票中。

The outer ring of Chengqilou is 72 metres in diameter, four storeys stretching 14 metres high and has 64 rooms on each floor. There are two staircases, one in the east and one in the west. The main entrance is at the south while side gates can be found on the east and west side of the Tulou. The second ring is mostly a single floor consisting of 36 rooms. Apart from the main and side gates, each small courtyard is connected to the next by corridors. The third ring is a single floor consisting of 20 rooms. In the past, in order to allow girls to be educated but also keeping them separated from the boys, a private school was opened here by the owner. The fourth ring is the main hall. It is a single floor covering an area of more than 30 square metres. It is at the core of the Tulou and signifies the head within the family. At the back of the hall, under the eaves and on the pillars, are inscriptions and couplets presented by famous persons, a practice since the Qing Dynasty.

Chengqilou covers an area of more than 5,300 square metres, with the outer ring being the tallest as they progressively get lower in height as you go inwards. It is tall, heavy, rugged and majestic in style with a long history and unique shape to make it the largest Tulou out of all the Yongding Tulou. This has earned it the status and reputation as the "Tulou King". Chengqinglou has since been included in countless Chinese prints and can be found on national stamps issued in China in 1986.

◎ 夜色承启楼。（陈军 摄）
The night scene of Chengqilou. (Photo by Chen Jun)

■ 世泽楼

　　从承启楼侧门出去大约10多米，便是方形土楼世泽楼。两楼之间距离很近，一方一圆，楼顶屋檐方圆结合，形成"方圆一线天"的独特景观。

　　世泽楼为高4层的四方形土楼，占地面积约5,100平方米，曾在民国年间毁于战火，上世纪三四十年代以传统工艺、材料按原状重建。楼内地势一阶比一阶高。四部楼梯分别设在楼的四个角上，全楼木制结构，不用一枚铁钉，整体线条流畅，立体层次感强，具有很高的艺术观赏价值。两口水井分别建在楼内东西两边，东边的称阳井，西边的称阴井。

■ Shizelou

About ten metres from the side gate of Chengqilou sits the square Shizelou. The distance between the two buildings is so close that the adjacent round and square roofs make a unique view of "a Sliver of the Sky".

Shizelou is a four storey Tulou with an area of about 5,100 square metres. It was severely damaged during the Chinese civil war but was later restored using traditional crafts and materials in the 1930s and 1940s. Within the square Tulou, each layer is higher than the next and there are staircases located in each corner. The wooden structure of the whole building does not need any nails, leaving smooth lines while still standing strong. A true artistic wonder with high appreciation value! A well can be found in the east, known as Yang Well, and another in the West known as Yin Well.

◎ 世泽楼。（王福平 摄）
Shizelou. (Photo by Wang Fuping)

© 方圆一线天。（王福平 摄）
A sliver of the sky. (Photo By Wang Fuping)

位于世泽楼东侧的是五云楼，高4层，占地面积约3,600平方米，迄今有500多年历史，是高北土楼群最古老的土楼，导游会趣称其为"土楼爷爷"。由于年代久远，五云楼的墙体呈现灰黄、白黄色，楼内木质结构也显得有些老旧，但仍然可以看出昔日的华丽装饰，脊顶飞檐翘角，厅内雕梁画栋，极为清幽雅致。

五云楼最大的特点是墙体没有砌石基，历经数百年风雨，墙体已向一侧倾斜，却没有倒塌，至今仍坚强地屹立在高北土楼群中，向世人展示她在福建土楼发展历史上的沧桑，所以也被人称为"不倒楼"，成为福建土楼的一大奇迹。

■ Wuyunlou

Located to the east of Shizelou with 4 storeys, Wuyunlou has a history of more than 500 years and covers an area of about 3,600 square metres. It is the oldest Tulou in the Gaobei Tulou Cluster. Tour guides often refer to it as the Grandfather Tulou. Due to its age, the colours of the wall are a mixture of a greyish yellow and white yellow; the wooden structure inside the building is also old and black. However, it adds to Wuyunlou's personality along with the carved beams within the hall giving it elegance and grace.

The most unique feature of Wuyunlou is that the wall has no stone foundation. After being battered by the weather for centuries, the wall has tilted to one side but has not yet collapsed. It still stands strong in the cluster and is a testament to the history and development of the Hakka Tulou. Therefore, Wuyunlou is often referred to as Never Falling Building and has become known as a bit of a miracle amongst Fujian Tulou.

◎ 五云楼。（胡家新 摄）
Wuyunlou. (Photo by Hu Jiaxin)

福建土楼

Fujian Tulou

◎ 博士楼。（胡家新 摄）
The Ph.D building. (Photo by Hu Jiaxin)

■ 侨福楼

高头村的江氏祖先建完五云楼以后，因家族人口越来越多，便先后建造了承启楼及世泽楼，世泽楼被战火摧毁并重建后不久，又陆陆续续建造了侨福楼等一批土楼，从而形成了今天的高北土楼群。

从承启楼西侧走出来不远，便能够看到一个洋气十足的大门，大门两边是一圈围墙，大门进去便是一个很宽敞的大院。年轻而又颇具特色的侨福楼便呈现在眼前。

侨福楼位于承启楼西侧，始建于1962年，占地面积2,300平方米。因为这座楼是海外的华侨出资兴建，再加上海内外江氏裔孙享用祖先庇佑的福气，所以叫作侨福楼，因这座楼出了11个博士的缘故，又被称为"博士楼"。

侨福楼也是中西合璧的土楼建筑，楼的大门和楼内的后厅都是西洋式的，厅堂正面有4根西式圆形石柱，内院以花岗石铺地。全楼结构是单环圆楼，高3层，中间为天井，因楼内原住居民大部分都在国外，所以天井没有任何建筑，这就让楼的整个空间变得宽敞起来，通风和采光都很好。全楼一口水井，东西两侧设有两部楼梯直通三楼。

◎ 家园。（胡家新 摄）

Home. (Photo by Hu Jiaxin)

■ Qiaofulou

After the Jiang family from Gaotou Village finished constructing Wuyunlou, they continued to build Chengqilou and Shizelou successively as a result of their growing family size. After Shizelou was damaged in the war it was rebuilt before construction of Qiaofulou started, therefore resulting in the formation of the Gaobei Tulou Cluster.

Not far from the west of Chengqilou is a Western style gate which is connected to a circular wall. Stepping through the gate will bring you to a very spacious compound, behold, the young and distinctive Qiaofulou.

Qiaofulou is located to the west of Chengqilou and was built in 1962. It covers an area of 2,300 square metres. Because this Tulou was funded by overseas Chinese and the Jiangs had descendants both domestically and internationally, the name of the Tulou is a representation of this diverse group. This building is also known as the Ph.D Building due to eleven members of this community achieving their doctorates.

Qiaofulou is a combination of both Chinese and Western styles. Four western style round stone pillars have been placed at the front of the hall while the inner courtyard is paved with granite. The whole building structure is a single ring. There are three floors and a patio in the middle. Most of the original residents in the building are abroad, so the patio has not been built upon, which is what makes the area so spacious allowing for good ventilation and lighting. There is only one water well in the whole building and two staircases, one in the east and one in the west.

◎ 侨福楼内景。（胡家新 摄）
The interiors of Qiaofulou. (Photo by Hu Jiaxin)

永定南溪土楼沟

永定区南溪土楼沟景区由数百座大小不一、形态各异的土楼组成。这些土楼依山就势、错落有致地分布在南溪河两岸，延绵十几千米，形成了一处蔚为壮观的"土楼长城"。其中列入《世界遗产名录》的有振福楼和衍香楼。

Tulougou Scenic Area in Nanxi

The hundreds of Tulou situated in Nanxi of Yongding District are of various sizes and shapes. These earth buildings are located on either bank of the Nanxi River, stretching for more than ten kilometres and forming the spectacular "Great Wall of Tulou". Out of the cluster, Zhenfulou and Yanxianglou were listed as World Cultural Heritage sites.

◎ 美丽的南溪土楼沟。（王福平 摄）
The amazing Tulou cluster. (Photo by Wang Fuping)

© 南溪沟的"土楼长城"。（陈成才 摄）
The "Great Wall of Tulou" at Nanxi. (Photo by Chen Chengcai)

■ 振福楼

　　"土楼长城"的起始点位于湖坑镇下南溪，古色古香的振福楼就在这里，因其拥有高贵典雅的气质，又被称为"土楼公主"。该楼与富丽堂皇的"土楼王子"振成楼之间有许多相似之处，而且两楼主人还有姻亲关系，所以振福楼跟振成楼可以称作"兄妹楼"。

　　振福楼建于1913年，占地面积4,000多平方米，共有3个厅堂，96个房间。楼前一条美丽的小溪，楼后是苍翠葱郁的高山，房屋周围青石小路四通八达。进入大门，便可看到一扇既有现代感又历经近百年历史的大铁门，其造型美观大方，连接之处全是用铆钉钉起来的，所以制作的难度特别大。进到楼内，可以明显感觉到冬暖夏凉的土楼里温度跟外面的差别。

◎ 归来。（赖永生 摄）

Coming home. (Photo by Lai Yongsheng)

◎ 门前小溪里戏水的娃娃们。（赖永生 摄）
Children playing in the creek. (Photo by Lai Yongsheng)

■ Zhenfulou

The starting point of the Tulou Great Wall is located in Nanxi of Hukeng Town. The quaint Zhenfulou sits here and because of its elegance, it is also known as the "Tulou Princess". There are many similarities between Zhenfulou and the "Tulou Prince", Zhenchenglou. In fact, the owners of these two Tulou have an in-law relationship so one could consider them brother and sister buildings.

Built in 1913, Zhenfulou covers an area of more than 4,000 square metres, with three halls and 96 rooms. A beautiful stream flows in front of the building while lush green mountains stand behind it. The stone trails around the residence extends in all directions. As you go through the main entrance gate, a large iron gate can be seen. It is both modern yet full of history extending almost a hundred years. It has a wonderful shape with the connectors made of rivets, making the production of this sort of gate particularly difficult. When entering the Tulou, you can feel the different temperature from outside as the particularly thick walls function as a heat insulator.

全楼由内外两环同心圆建筑组成。外环高3层、11米,墙厚1.6米,分别有4部楼梯通向二、三楼。内环单层,两面坡瓦屋顶,而且有很多精美的装饰,所以被称作是"外土内洋"。内环前向的门俗称内门,雕梁画栋,琉璃瓦面,石质门框镌刻对联,门两边为砖雕花格窗棂。

后厅与两侧回廊、中厅(厅堂)围合,自成院落,前面为天井。有时在天井可以看到几只乌龟爬来爬去,是楼主用来疏通下水道的"清洁工",因为乌龟会沿着下水道爬行,可以疏通管道里的淤泥和树叶。

如今,振福楼内设立了"客家家风楼",通过展板、影像、匾额等形式展示了土楼客家名人、客家山歌俗语、客家民俗等反映出的家风故事,展示了客家人孝悌、忠信、礼义、廉耻的精神内涵。

◎ 振福楼内门。(张耀辉 摄)
The front door of the inner ring. (Photo by Zhang Yaohui)

◎ 精美装饰的厅堂。（赖永生 摄）
The decorated hall. (Photo by Lai Yongsheng)

The entire Tulou consists of two concentric circles. The outer ring has three storeys and is 11 metres high with a 1.6-metre-thick wall. There are four staircases leading to the second and third floors. The inner ring has one single floor with two sloping roofs and many beautiful decorations. Some say you should not judge a book by its cover because while the outer wall may be made of earth, its interior is wonderfully adorned. The front door of the inner ring has a painted and carved beam, a glazed tile surface, and an engraved door frame. The two sides are a lattice of carved brick.

The back hall encloses a self-contained area with corridors on either side and the middle hall. There is a patio at the front where one can stand and watch a few turtles crawl around. These turtles tend to crawl along the sewers which helps prevent blockage by silt and leaves.

Nowadays, Zhenfulou is known to be where to immerse oneself in Hakka family tradition education. It has been divided into several parts: gratefulness, filial piety, farming, diligence and honesty. It passes on many stories of family values such as loyalty and benevolence. They embody the Hakka community's traditions and culture.

■ 衍香楼

衍香楼位于新南村南溪河与奥杏溪的汇合之处，背靠高耸的青山，周边是形状各异的土楼。山水、土楼、古桥交相辉映，风景别致生动。

衍香楼建于1842年，高3层，占地面积约4,300平方米，外环为圆楼，里面一座方形院落，外圆内方，圆中有方，是福建土楼中风格较为独特的土楼。大门上镌刻着"大夫第"三个字，可见楼主人是名门望族，曾经出过达官显要。大楼的楼门上方可见"衍香楼"三个苍劲有力的大字，门扇外封铁板，门楣上方设有防火水槽，以防火攻。

衍香楼的内厅为仿府第式建筑，雕梁画栋、古朴典雅，梁柱间"群龙腾云""卧狮踞梁"等木雕栩栩如生，墙壁上书画精美、龙飞凤舞，枋额斗拱有"五福临门"、花鸟虫鱼等艳丽多姿的彩绘。这些技艺超凡的雕刻和绘画，烘托出了这个历代以诗书传家的书香门第。全楼整体布局协调、统一、美观而实用。

楼旁有一个绿树成荫、古木参天的后花园。静静地走在幽静的小路上，依稀听见小鸟扑打翅膀的声音和绿竹叶被风轻轻吹过的声音。楼后古老的石头路，连着几处破旧的房子和残垣断壁的土楼，令人心生感慨。

我国著名城市规划专家、古建筑保护专家郑孝燮考察此楼后，题诗一首：

远山近水土圆楼，隔壁残垣且伴留。耕读传家犹传世，诗情画境何悠悠。

◎ 如画衍香楼。（赖永生 摄）

Picturesque Yanxianglou. (By Lai Yongsheng)

◎ 楼内主厅。（赖永生 摄）

The hall in Yanxianglou. (Photo by Lai Yongsheng)

■ Yanxianglou

Yanxianglou is situated at the junction of Nanxi River and Aoyao Stream, surrounded by towering green hills, flowing water, ancient bridges and other Tulou, making it an astounding scene to behold.

Built in 1842, Yanxianglou has three storeys and covers an area of about 4,300 square metres. It is made up of an outer ring and a square courtyard, a unique combination. Signage shows the characters "大夫第" indicating that the residents of this building may have been a well-known family. The big bold characters of Yanxianglou can be seen above the buildings door. Iron plates have been placed on the doors while a fire prevention water tank can be found above the door.

The inner hall of Yanxianglou has carved beams and elegant paintings. The wooden carvings featured inside seem to be alive while the paintings on the walls depict dancing dragons and phoenixes, crouching lions, flowers, birds and insects—a swirl of brilliant colours. These exquisite art on the walls brings alive poems written by past generations. The overall layout of the whole building is coordinated, unified, beautiful and practical.

Next to the building is a tree-lined, old-fashioned back garden. Its serenity allows one to hear bird wings flapping as they fly and the gentle rustle of bamboo leaves being blown by the wind. Behind the building is an ancient stone road. Here, one can find several dilapidated houses and rustic Tulou. It would seem that the whole Yanxianglou is a scene that would inspire poets.

Zheng Xiaoxie, a famous expert in urban planning and ancient architecture preservation, visited this Yanxianglou and reflected by writing a poem describing nature and history's existence side by side.

◎ 残垣伴留。（冯木波 摄）

Nature and history's coexistence. (Photo by Feng Mubo)

南靖田螺坑土楼群

　　从龙岩市永定区高北土楼群到漳州市南靖县田螺坑土楼群大约20千米。列入《世界遗产名录》的田螺坑土楼群由五座保存完好的土楼组成，分别为方形的步云楼，圆形的振昌楼、瑞云楼、和昌楼和椭圆形的文昌楼。五座土楼坐落在海拔787.8米的湖崇山半山坡上，三面环山，前面是美丽的梯田。四座圆形土楼依山势起伏，高低错落，疏密有致，远远看去，就像装着菜的四个圆盘子，而方楼步云楼位于四座圆形土楼中间，构成一幅具有强烈视觉冲击力的美妙景观，因此被誉为"四菜一汤"，名扬天下。

　　著名古建筑专家罗哲文先生曾为田螺坑土楼群题诗一首：

　　　　田螺坑畔土楼家，雾散云开映彩霞。
　　　　俯视宛如花一朵，旁看神似布达拉。
　　　　或云天外飞来碟，亦说鲁班墨斗花。
　　　　似此楼形世罕见，环球建苑一奇葩。

◎ 土楼群俯视图。（章庆煌 摄）
An aerial view of the Tulou cluster. (Photo by Zhang Qinghuang)

◎ 土楼群仰视图。（朱庆福 摄）

An upward view of the Tulou cluster. (Photo by Zhu Qingfu)

Tianluokeng Tulou Cluster in Nanjing

There is about 20 kilometres between Yongding Gaobei Tulou Cluster and Tianluokeng Tulou Cluster of Nanjing, Zhangzhou . The latter consists of five well-preserved Tulou, namely the square Buyunlou, the circular Zhenchanglou, Ruiyunlou, Hechanglou and the oval Wenchanglou. These Tulou are located on the slope of Hudong Mountain at an altitude of 787.8 metres and are surrounded by mountains on three sides. The square Buyunlou sits in the middle of the four circular Tulou. Some say that this looks like a Chinese dinner table with four round dishes of food and one square bowl of soup in the middle.

Famous ancient architect expert, Luo Zhewen, once wrote a poem for Tianluokeng Tulou Cluster commenting on its peculiar location amongst the fog and clouds, comparing them to a flower and UFOs.

■ 步云楼

田螺坑土楼群中间的方楼叫步云楼，建于清代1662至1722年间。据当地黄氏族谱记载，其祖先黄百三郎从龙岩永定移居田螺坑，利用茂密丛林和遍地田螺养鸭，修得此楼。1936年被匪烧毁，于1953年在旧址重建。

步云楼坐东北朝西南，占地面积1,050平方米，建筑面积1,393平方米。楼高3层，每层26个房间，第一层为厨房，第二层为谷仓，第三层为卧室。4部楼梯分别设在楼内的四个角落，每层楼的通道都是相通的。

从步云楼的大门进去，淳朴热情的土楼人，一边忙着手中的活，一边热情地招呼来往的游客。楼内因为地势太高无法挖井，所以该楼的水井设在楼外，并且在水井周围砌了一条排水沟。天井自外向内根据高低地势分三级台阶，一个台阶比一个台阶高，走上去有种步步高升的感觉，故而该楼取名步云楼，寓意子孙后代平步青云、步步高升。

◎ "四菜一汤"中心的汤。（冯木波 摄）
The square "bowl of soup" in the middle. (Photo by Feng Mubo)

■ Buyunlou

Buyunlou is the square building situated in the middle of the cluster. It was built during 1662—1722 of the Qing Dynasty by the residents' ancestor Huang. According to the local Huang genealogy, an ancestor moved from Yongding District of Longyan to Tianluokeng. Here, in the dense forests was an abundance of snails which he used as food to raise ducks. This move eventually led to the construction of Buyunlou. Unfortunately, it was burnt down in 1936 due to arson, but was rebuilt in 1953.

Buyunlou sits in the northeast while facing southwest. It covers a land area of 1,050 square metres while the building itself has an area of 1,393 square metres. The building has three floors and 26 rooms per floor. The first floor is the kitchen, the second floor is the granary and the third floor is where you will find the bedrooms. There are four staircases located in the four corners of the buildings. The corridors on each floor go all the way around.

Upon entering Buyunlou, the welcoming residents show warmth as they go about their day. Having a water well outside the building with a drainage ditch built around it is essential due to the location of the building on high terrain. The patio is divided into three levels in accordance with the terrain, with one slightly rising above the other. This feature is reflected in the name of the Tulou as if there are steps in the clouds. The ancestors hoped that their descendants would continue learning and rising above.

◎ 寓意平步青云的天井。（冯木波 摄）
The patio featured continue rising up. (Photo by Feng Mubo)

■ 振昌楼

步云楼的西侧即左下方是圆形土楼振昌楼，始建于1930年。该楼坐东北朝西南，占地面积976平方米，建筑面积1,232平方米，楼高3层，每层26个房间，设2部楼梯。

振昌楼的楼门比较小，跨过门槛进入天井，鹅卵石铺成的天井中间有两座小木屋，一口水井。若是在炎热的夏日，你能看到楼里的孩子们，从井里打上一桶水，喝上几口，再把剩余的水浇在腿上脚上，顿时一股清凉。环顾四围，楼内的墙壁和楼板都已经被炊烟熏黑了。院子里的鸡鸭猫狗，似乎已经习惯了来来往往的游客，在土楼里悠闲自得地溜达着。

■ Zhenchanglou

To the west of Buyunlou is the circular Zhenchanglou which sits slightly lower and began to be built in 1930. It faces the southwest and covers a land area of 976 square metres while the building is 1,232 square metres. The building has three storeys with 26 rooms on each floor and two staircases.

Zhenchanglou is relatively small. Crossing the gate and into the patio, you can see two cabins and a well. If it is a hot summer, you may see some children of the Tulou fetching water from the well, drinking from the bucket and then pouring the cool water on their bodies. Looking around, the walls and floors seem to have been blackened by smoke. Various animals can be seen strolling around the building. It seems that they have become accustomed to visitors as they continue about their day despite the coming and goings.

◎ 静静的振昌楼。（冯木波 摄）
The quiet Zhenchanglou. (Photo by Feng Mubo)

■ 瑞云楼

步云楼的东南侧即右下方是圆形土楼瑞云楼，建于1936年，占地面积1,063平方米，建筑面积1,176平方米，高3层，每层26个房间，共84个房间，设2部楼梯，1个大门，1口水井。

进入大门以后向前方仰望，可以看到后面最高的和昌楼。楼内居民生活井然有序，主人总是热情地招呼着来客。如果有兴趣，可以在土楼里和主人们一起共进晚餐，品尝农家美食，再一起享受漫天繁星的静谧夜空。

◎ 夜幕下的瑞云楼。（胡家新 摄）
Ruiyunlou at dusk. (Photo by Hu Jiaxin)

■ Ruiyunlou

To the southeast and lower right of Buyunlou, is the rotund Ruiyunlou. Built in 1936, it covers an area of 1,063 square metres of land while the building is 1,176 square metres in area. It has three storeys and with 26 rooms per floor, there are a total of 84 rooms. There are two staircases, one gate and one well.

When you are inside Ruiyunlou, you can see Hechanglou which sits at the very top. The residents of Ruiyunlou are always cheerful and welcome visitors with open arms. If you are interested, you can even have dinner hosted by one of the residents and enjoy the tranquil environment together.

■ 和昌楼

土楼群里最高处的是和昌楼，始建于元末明初约1354年，原为方楼，后遭匪患，于1953年在原址上改建为土木结构的圆楼。该楼坐东北朝西南，占地面积1,268平方米，建筑面积1,658平方米，楼高3层，每层22间。全楼只有一个大门，设两部楼梯。从大门进去便可看到天井有一个古老小木屋和一口水井，内院以鹅卵石铺地。每层楼上都挂着大红灯笼，非常喜气。

站在和昌楼的大门口，其他4座土楼一览无余。远远望去，弯弯曲曲的盘山公路一直延伸到山里，大山深处云雾缭绕，山川秀美，梯田层层，与错落有致的土楼构成一幅美丽的水墨画。

◎ 最高处的和昌楼。（冯木波 摄）

Hechanglou located at the highest point. (Photo by Feng Mubo)

◎ 大喜的日子。（冯木波 摄）

During a wedding celebration. (Photo by Feng Mubo)

■ Hechanglou

Located at the highest point out of all the Tulou in the cluster, Hechanglou was built around 1354. It was originally a square building but was changed to a round building in 1953 during reconstruction. It sits in the northeast and faces southwest. It covers a land area of 1,268 square metres while the building itself has an area of 1,658 square metres. There are three floors and 22 rooms per floor. There is only one main entrance to the Tulou and two staircases. From the entrance, you can see an old wooden cabin and a well. The inner courtyard is paved with pebbles. Red lanterns line each floor, livening up the atmosphere.

Standing at the gate of Hechanglou, the other four earth buildings can be seen unobstructed. From afar, a winding path disappears into the misty mountains as it draws your attention to the breathtaking view before you. With layered terraces, earthen buildings, mountains and rivers, it makes the perfect scene for a painting.

■ 文昌楼

　　位于步云楼西南侧的是文昌楼，一座建于1966年的椭圆形土楼，占地面积1,288平方米，建筑面积2,210平方米，楼高3层，每层32个房间。设2部楼梯，1个大门，1口水井。

　　文昌楼虽然是5座土楼中最年轻的一座，却是建筑面积最大的土楼。穿过用厚杉木铁皮制作的大门，便可以看到露天的大天井，一排排房门和窗户都朝着天井的方向。楼顶层外墙有3个瞭望台和4个射击口。

■ Wenchanglou

Located behind Buyunlou, Wenchanglou is an oval shaped Tulou built in 1966. The building itself has an area of 2,210 square metres and covers a land area of 1,288 square metres. There are three floors, 32 rooms per floor, 2 staircases, one entrance gate and one well.

Although Wenchanglou is the youngest of the five Tulou, it is the largest in terms of building area. Entering the gate made out of iron-clad fir wood, you can see the large open-air courtyard. Rows of doors and windows face the uneven courtyard. The top floor of the Tulou has three lookouts and four firing ports.

◎ 椭圆形的文昌楼。（胡家新 摄）
The oval shaped Wenchanglou. (Photo by Hu Jiaxin)

游览田螺坑的"四菜一汤"土楼，一定不能错过有些魔幻的土楼夜景。夜幕降临，土楼里悬挂的灯笼全部点亮，楼外的射灯在土楼外墙洒上一层朦胧的亮光，轮廓清晰的土楼群在夜色中显得格外迷人壮观。

The magical night view of the "four dishes one soup" Tulou of Tianluokeng. As night falls, the lanterns light up the Tulou, providing a clear outline of each earthen building, showing off its subtle charm.

◎ 欢乐的土楼之夜。（冯木波 摄）
Joyful celebrations at Tianluokeng Tulou Cluster (Photo by Feng Mubo)

南靖河坑土楼群

　　河坑土楼群位于福建省漳州市南靖县书洋镇曲江村河坑自然村，距南靖县城58千米，由方形的朝水楼、阳照楼、永贵楼、永盛楼、永荣楼、绳庆楼和圆形的春贵楼、裕兴楼、裕昌楼、永庆楼、晓春楼、东升楼及五角形的南薰楼共13座土楼组成。该土楼群东、西、南三面青山环绕，北面曲江溪绿水流过。站在河坑村的狮子山山顶，远远看去，土楼群如天上的"北斗七星"般排列开来，所以河坑土楼群又有"仙山楼阁""北斗七星"之称，形成美景天成、天人合一的奇观。

　　河坑土楼群中最古老的朝水楼，由张氏祖先始建于1549年，后子孙繁衍，在这个不足一平方千米的山间溪畔，建起了一座又一座土楼，土楼群成为福建土楼分布最密集的楼群。其中最年轻的永庆楼，建成于20世纪60年代。整个土楼群的建造时间足足跨越了420多年。

◎ 春日河坑。（冯木波　摄）
The cluster in spring. (Photo by Feng Mubo)

Hekeng Tulou Cluster in Nanjing

Hekeng Tulou Cluster is located in Hekeng Village, Shuyang Town in Zhangzhou City. There are 13 Tulou of both square and circular shapes. This cluster is surrounded by green hills on the east, west and south while the Qujiang Stream flows through the north. Hekeng Tulou Cluster sometimes can be referred to as the big dipper. This is because the cluster can be seen from afar at the top of Hekeng Village's Lion Mountain and looks like the big dipper constellation.

The cluster is of Fujian's most densely populated Tulou. The Zhang's ancestors began to build Chaoshuilou around 1549, followed by Tulou being built one after another until Yongqinglou was completed in the 1960s. A time of over 420 years has witnessed the formation of the cluster.

◎ 彩霞映照下的土楼群。（冯木波 摄）
The cluster under rosy clouds. (Photo by Feng Mubo)

■ 春贵楼

春贵楼位于河坑桥村口,是进入河坑古村落的第一座土楼。该楼坐西南朝东北,建于1963至1968年,占地面积为1,808平方米,建筑面积3,304平方米,楼高3层,每层32个房间,4部相互对称的楼梯。

因为著名电视节目《爸爸去哪儿》拍摄时明星入住春贵楼,这座土楼也成了明星土楼,很多游客慕名前来,到水井旁打水,与天井中架起的晾衣竹竿合影,探寻村民独特的生活用具等等。土楼里原生态的生活气息,深深地吸引着他们。

■ Chunguilou

The circular Chunguilou is located at the entrance to the village. It is also the first Tulou to be seen as you approach this area. Sitting in the southwest and facing north east, Chunguilou was built from 1963 to 1968. It covers a land area of 1,808 square metres while the building has an area of 3,304 square metres. There are three storeys, 32 rooms on each floor and four symmetrical staircases.

The very popular TV program "*Dad, where are we going?*' was once shoot in Hekeng Tulou Cluster, and famous actors lived in Chunguilou. This made this Tulou a star and attract countless tourists. They are fascinated by the original aspects of the residents' lifestyle and have much fun drawing water from the well, taking pictures with the bamboo poles for hanging clothes on in the patio, and exploring living facilities of the Zhang's families.

◎ 原汁原味的生活。(冯木波 摄)
Original lifestyle. (Photo by Feng Mubo)

◎ 春贵楼内景。（冯木波 摄）

The interior of Chunguilou. (Photo by Feng Mubo)

■ 裕兴楼

从春贵楼旁边的一条石头路沿着溪流往上走，紧挨着春贵楼的便是裕兴楼。这座圆形土楼建于1969至1971年，坐西朝东，占地面积907平方米，建筑面积1,959平方米，楼高3层，每层20个房间，1个大门，2部对称的楼梯。

裕兴楼是河坑土楼群最年轻的土楼之一，大小约为裕昌楼的一半。该楼没有水井，以前楼内需要用水的时候要到隔壁的裕昌楼挑水。楼内很多村民都是从裕昌楼搬过来的，所以两座楼有点像"父子楼"。

◎ 谜一样的世界。（冯木波 摄）
A riddle-like world. (Photo by Feng Mubo)

■ Yuxinglou

Following a stone path next to Chunguilou, walk up the river to arrive at Yuxinglou. This circular Tulou was built between 1969 and 1971. It sits in the west and faces the east covering a land area of 907 square metres. The building itself is 1,959 square metres and has three storeys, 20 rooms per floor, one gate and two mirroring staircases.

Yuxinglou is one of the youngest Tulou in this cluster, and is about half the size of Yuchanglou. There is no well in this Tulou. When water was needed, the residents have to go next door to Yuchanglou where they had come from, and as a result, the locals will say these two Tulou are like father and son.

■ 裕昌楼

从裕兴楼出来往右走一点就可以看到旁边的裕昌楼，它跟书洋镇下坂村的裕昌楼，即著名的"东歪西斜楼"同名，两座土楼却各有千秋。裕昌楼是一座建于1943至1947年的圆形土楼。该楼坐西北朝东南，占地面积1,838平方米，建筑面积3,609平方米。楼高3层，每层36个房间，共108个房间，设4部楼梯，1个大门，内院右侧有1口水井。

裕昌楼楼名上方有一幅精美的图案，中间还有一个鲜艳的五角星。从土楼的大门进去，迎面是一个别有洞天的大广场，这个平坦而又宽阔的天井没有什么建筑，地面全部都是石头铺就，土楼居民或者游客可以自由自在地在这里走走停停、停停走走。

裕昌楼、裕兴楼、春贵楼排成一列，屹立在涓涓流过的小溪旁、河坑桥的入口处，像是守门人守护着这个土楼群，守护着这个原生态的古村落。

◎ 别具特色的大门。（冯木波 摄）

A characteristic gate. (Photo by Feng Mubo)

■ Yuchanglou

Yuchanglou and Yuxinglou are situated side by side. Although it shares the same name as the Yuchanglou in Xiaban Village, Shuyang Town, they are very different. Yuchanglou is a circular Tulou built between 1943 and 1947. It faces southeast and covers a land area of 1,838 square metres. The Tulou itself measures 3,609 square metres. There are three floors, 36 rooms per floor, four staircases, one main entrance gate and a well that can be found on the right side of the inner courtyard.

Above the name plate of Yuchanglou, there is a beautiful symbol and a conspicuous five-pointed star. In the Tulou is an open patio. The ground is paved with stone and anyone can walk around freely.

Yuchanglou, Yuxinglou and Chunguilou all line up in a row next to the flowing stream and Hekeng Bridge. They are the gatekeepers of the cluster, guarding the village that is their special home.

◎ 平坦宽阔的天井。（冯木波 摄）
The wide open patio. (Photo by Feng Mubo)

■ 朝水楼

朝水楼是河坑土楼群中最中间的方形土楼，建于明代1549至1553年间，坐北朝南，占地面积729平方米，建筑面积1,890平方米，楼高3层，每层20个房间，只有2部楼梯。

该楼特色之一是古老，是河坑土楼群中最古老的土楼，距今已有400多年的历史。二是无石砌墙基，为福建土楼中现存不多的无石砌墙基土楼之一。从大门进去，可见天井里面有一口水井，后厅不在正中间，比起其他土楼显得有些特别。无论是斑驳粗糙的墙面还是楼内古老陈旧的物件，无不见证着这座土楼的沧桑，见证着土楼人家祖祖辈辈聚族而居的场景，见证着这座大山山谷里原汁原味的土楼生活。

◎ 400岁的古老土楼。（冯木波 摄）
The ancient Tulou of 400 years old. (Photo by Feng Mubo)

■ Chaoshuilou

Chaoshuilou is a square Tulou located towards the middle of the cluster. Built during the Ming Dynasty between 1549 and 1553, Chaoshuilou faces the north. Covering a land area of 729 square metres, the building itself has an area of 1,890 square metres. It has three floors with 20 rooms per floor and only two staircases.

One key feature of this Tulou is its age. It is the oldest Tulou in the Hekeng Tulou Cluster having experienced more than 400 years of history. Another key feature is its stone-free wall foundation, making it one of the rare few that have such a structure. Walking into the courtyard, you will see a water well and that the back hall is not located in the centre where it usually is. The layout is particularly different from other Tulou. Whether it is an aging wall or an antique object within the building, one can witness all that the Tulou has lived through. Every detail tells a story about the life of those who have lived in this earthen building.

■ 阳照楼

阳照楼位于朝水楼西侧，是一座建于清光绪元年（1875）的方形土楼。该楼坐西南朝东北，占地面积1,156平方米,建筑面积2,775平方米。楼高3层，每层26个房间，共78个房间，设4部楼梯，1个大门。

从大门进去，便可以见到楼内的厅堂，厅堂两旁是排列整齐的房间。夏日，大门前面的一口池塘里荷叶满塘，荷花绽放，恰似楼内居民安居乐业的生活，宁静而美好。

◎ 建于清代的阳照楼。（冯木波 摄）
Yangzhaolou built in the Qing Dynasty. (Photo by Feng Mubo)

◎ 楼名倒映在门前的荷塘里。（冯木波 摄）

The reflection of the name in the lotus-covered pond . (Photo by Feng Mubo)

■ Yangzhaolou

Located on Chaoshuilou's west side, Yangzhaolou is a square Tulou built in 1875 of the Qing Dynsaty. It sits in the southwest and faces northeast. It has a land area of 1,156 square metres while the building area is 2,775 square metres. There are three floors, each with 26 rooms, four staircases and one main entrance gate. There is also a pond in front of the gate.

As you step through the main entrance, a hall greets you in the middle, its sides lined neatly with rooms. In summer, the pond in front of the Tulou is always filled with lush green lotus leaves with flowers blooming, like the residents' life here, quiet and beautiful.

◎ 永贵楼门前。（冯木波 摄）
In front of Yongguilou. (Photo by Feng Mubo)

■ 永贵楼

　　永贵楼位于朝水楼北侧，是一座建于清光绪二年（1876）的方形土楼。该楼坐南朝北，占地面积1,680平方米,建筑面积3,852平方米，主楼高3层10.29米。大门上方镶嵌一方楼名石刻，楼名旁边标有建筑该楼的明确纪年。

　　从永贵楼大门进去，楼内天井建有一排三间的厅堂，砖木结构，秀美简朴，厅堂中间为观音厅，旁边两个房间用于住宿和吃饭。整个天井地面都是用石头铺成，石头之间布满绿色的青苔，给人一种久远的年代感。

■ Yongguilou

Yongguilou is located to the north of Chaoshuilou. It is a square Tulou built in 1876 of the Qing Dynasty. The building sits in the south and faces the north covering a land area of 1,680 square metres. The building itself is 3,014 square metres. The main part of the building has three floors and is 10.29 metres high. Clearly engraved above the buildings main entrance is its name and the year it was built.

Stepping inside, there is a row of three halls in the inner courtyard. The brick and wood structure is simple yet stunning. The middle hall is known as Guanyin Hall while the two on the side are used for accommodation and meals. The entire courtyard is made of stones which are covered in the slightest layer of green moss, adding to the historical feel.

■ 永庆楼

　　永庆楼位于朝水楼南侧，是一座建于1967至1972年的圆形土楼。该楼坐南朝北，占地面积1,661平方米，建筑面积3,138平方米，楼高3层，每层32个房间，楼内只有2部楼梯，1个大门，1口水井。

　　永庆楼大门外，一派美丽的田园风光，翠绿的田野和这朴实无华的土楼相映成趣。走在土楼旁边的乡间小道上，一边吹着清新的空气，一边欣赏着或远或近的土楼，这古老幽静的村落，苍翠的山川田野，清澈的小溪以及热情质朴的村民，不禁让人心旷神怡。

■ Yongqinglou

Yongqinglou is located south of Chaoshuilou. It is circular and built between 1967 and 1972. It sits in the south and faces the north. Covering a land area of 1,661 square metres, the building itself has an area of 3,138 square metres. It is three storeys high with 32 rooms per floor, has two staircases, one main gate and one well.

Outside the gate is a beautiful scenery of verdant fields and quaint Tulou. A fresh breeze gently caresses those walking through the countryside admiring the surroundings next to the Tulou. This ancient and quiet village with green hills and clear rivers is home to villagers who are full of warmth and kindness.

◎ 丰收的喜悦。（冯木波 摄）
Celebrating the harvest. (Photo by Feng Mubo)

◎ 日复一日。（冯木波 摄）

Day in and day out. (Photo by Feng Mubo)

■ 晓春楼

建于1967至1970年的圆形土楼晓春楼，坐东朝西，占地面积1,808平方米，建筑面积3,833平方米，楼高3层，每层32个房间。有1个大门，1个前厅和1个后厅。

晓春楼门前有一块平地，一条小溪连着几座土楼。楼内是一个宽敞的天井，楼内村民随意散放着各种生活用具。偌大的土楼却只有2部对称的楼梯，更能够让人想象土楼人家自由连通、和谐共处的生活场景。

■ Xiaochunlou

Xiaochunlou is a circular Tulou built between 1967 and 1970. Sitting in the east and facing the west, it covers a land area of 1,808 square metres. The building itself is 3,833 square metres with three floors, each with 32 rooms, and one main entrance. There is a front hall and back hall.

The terrain in front of Xiaochunlou is flat. A small creek runs between several of the Tulou. Inside the structure is a spacious patio where villagers are free to use a variety of everyday tools. There are only two staircases mirroring one another which makes it possible to imagine the coexistence of the Tulou people in a connected and harmonious space.

■ 永盛楼

永盛楼位于晓春楼的对面，是一座建于清1662年至1722年的方形土楼，坐南朝北，占地面积676平方米，建筑面积2,128平方米，楼高4层14.4米，每层34个房间。设4部楼梯，1个大门，墙厚1.4米，院内有一口水井。永盛楼虽然也是一座占地面积较小的方形土楼，却是河坑土楼群中层数最多、楼高最高的土楼。

■ Yongshenglou

Located opposite Xiaochunlou, Yongshenglou is a square Tulou built in the Qing Dymasty between 1662 and 1722. It faces the north and sits on a land area of 676 square metres. The building is 2,128 square metres and is four storeys high, standing 14.4 metres in height. Each floor has thirty-four rooms. There are four staircases and one entrance gate. The walls are 1.4 metres thick and a well can be found in the inner courtyard. Although Yongshenglou takes up little space, it has the most number of floors and is the tallest within the Hekeng Tulou Cluster.

◎ 永盛楼和它的邻居们。（冯木波 摄）
Yongshenglou and its neighbors. (Photo by Feng Mubo)

◎ 盆景点缀的庭院。（冯木波 摄）
The patio decorated with bonsai. (Photo by Feng Mubo)

■ 永荣楼

　　永荣楼位于永盛楼西侧，是一座建于1736至1795年的方形土楼，占地525平方米，建筑面积1,377平方米，楼高3层，每层设置18个房间，设4部楼梯，1个大门。

　　永荣楼跟其他土楼不一样的是楼门开在正面墙的右侧，没有后厅，正对着大门的一边土楼由于失火重建，至今还没有建好，3层的木结构没有围栏和木板，可以看出其最原始的建筑。永荣楼是河坑土楼群最小的一座土楼，小小天井里的水井布满了青苔，楼里的老人爱美，在院子里种上了一些盆景，让简陋古老的土楼有了别样生机。

■ Yongronglou

Yongronglou is located on the west side of Yongshenglou. It is a square Tulou built between 1736 and 1795. The land area it covers is 525 square metres but the building's area is 1,377 square metres. There are three storeys with 18 rooms on each floor, four staircases and one main entrance gate.

Where Yongronglou differs from other Tulou is that the main entrance is located to the right of the main wall face, and there is no back hall. Part of the wall was damaged during a fire and has yet be rebuilt. The three-storey wooden structure has no fencing or wooden boards, exhibiting one of the most primitive Tulou in the world. Yongronglou is the smallest Tulou in the cluster, thus, there is only one moss-covered well and a small patio. Though this building looks very old, the residents beautified their environment with several bonsai.

■ 东升楼

　　东升楼紧挨着晓春楼，两座楼之间大约有十余米，是一座建于1958至1961年的圆形土楼。该楼坐东朝西，占地面积870平方米，建筑面积2,063平方米，楼高3层，每层22个房间、1个大门、1口水井。

　　东升楼是河坑土楼群较大的圆形土楼，走进大门，迎面而来的是一个宽阔的天井。热情好客的村民讲着一口纯正的客家话，满脸笑容。楼后面翠绿的田野从远而近传来美妙的鸟鸣声，让人久久不愿离去。

■ Dongshenglou

Dongshenglou can be found about 10 metres next to Xiaochunlou. It is a circular Tulou built during 1958 to 1961. The Tulou sits in the east and faces the west, covering a land area of 870 square metres, while the building's area is 2,063 square metres. There are three storeys with 22 rooms per floor, one main entrance gate and one well.

Dongshenglou is a large circular Tulou in a cluster. As you step through the gate, there is a large patio. The hospitable villagers will greet you with smiles and welcome you in Hakka. The mesmerising sound of singing birds floats in from the green fields behind the Tulou, making visitors reluctant to leave.

◎ 恬静的小院。（冯木波 摄）
　The peaceful building. (Photo by Feng Mubo)

■ **南薰楼**

从东升楼出来沿着小溪旁边的小路往上行走大约100余米，即可见到南薰楼。这是一座建于1821至1850年的土楼，该楼坐北朝南，占地面积729平方米，建筑面积1,758平方米，楼高3层，每层21间，共63间，设4部楼梯，1个大门。

这座楼有两个特色，一是由于楼门朝向被改以后，厅堂变成位于土楼的右侧，成为南靖县境内唯一一座厅堂在楼右侧的土楼。另外一个特色就是这幢土楼由于用地限制，有一个墙角由直角砌成钝角，呈五角形态，让这座土楼成为福建世遗土楼中唯一的一座五角形土楼。

■ **Nanxunlou**

If you follow the river from Dongshenglou for about 100 metres, you will arrive at Nanxunlou. Built between 1821 and 1850, Nanxunlou faces the south and covers a land area of 729 square metres. The building itself has an area of 1,758 square metres. There are three storeys with 21 rooms on each floor, four staircases and one main gate.

There are two key characteristics about Nanxunlou. First is the position of the hall within the Tulou. After the main gate was renovated, the hall's position is now to the right, making it the first of its kind within Nanjing County. The second characteristic is that one of the corners is at an obtuse angle, making Nanxunlou the only Tulou in a pentagonal shape on the World Heritage List.

◎ 位于土楼右侧的厅堂。（冯木波 摄）
The hall located on the right side. (Photo by Feng Mubo)

◎ 绳庆楼内景。（冯木波 摄）

The interiors of Shengqinglou. (Photo by Feng Mubo)

■ 绳庆楼

　　绳庆楼位于河坑土楼群的最东端，是一座建于1723至1735年的方形土楼，坐东朝西，占地2,310平方米。整座楼有上下2个天井，3个大门，1个侧门。

　　绳庆楼形状呈"日"字形，颇有特色，绳庆楼呈"口"字的主楼前低后高，前排是高3层12米，后排3层半，厅堂建于天井前排连接后厅的地方，堂内和墙壁上可以看到古老精美的木雕装饰和花草图案彩绘。楼外呈"口"字形的是附楼，建于20世纪40年代末，高2层8米，主楼和附楼被高低错落有致的三面墙围合起来，形成厝包楼、楼包厝的奇妙景观。

■ Shengqinglou

Located towards the eastern side of the Hekeng Tulou Cluster, Shengqinglou is square in shape and built between 1723 and 1735. It faces the west and covers a land area of 2,310 square metres. The entire building has two patios, three gates and one side door.

The shape of Shengqinglou looks like the Chinese character for sun ("日"). The main structure of Shengqinglou is low at the front and high at the back. The front has three storeys and has a height of 12 metres, while the rear has three and half levels. The hall was built where the patio in the front connects to the back hall. On the walls are fine antique wood carvings with flower motifs. A square annex building can be located outside the Tulou. It was constructed in the late 1940s and stands 8 metres high. The main structure and the annex building are surrounded by three walls and creates a wonderful landscape to see.

南靖云水谣景区

在云水谣景区山脚下、溪岸旁、田野上，星罗棋布着一座座姿态万千的土楼。这些土楼从13世纪元朝中期开始建造，目前保存完好的有53座。其中被列入《世界遗产名录》的，有建在沼泽地上堪称"天下第一奇"的和贵楼，有工艺精美、保护完好的双环圆形土楼怀远楼。此外，还有吊脚楼、竹竿楼、府第式土楼等，土楼风景别具一格。

◎ 撒网。（胡家新 摄）
Casting the net. (Photo by Hu Jiaxin)

◎ 在水一方。（冯木波 摄）

The riverside Tulou. (By Feng Mubo)

Yunshuiyao Scenic Area in Nanjing

At Yunshuiyao Scenic Area many differently shaped Tulou buildings are scattered at the foot of the mountain, lining the bank of the river and sitting alongside fields. There are 53 well-preserved Tulou that have existed since the 13th century. Two of them can be found on UNESCO's World Heritage List, including Heguilou on marshland, known for being a wonder of the world, and the double-ringed Huaiyuanlou, known for its well-crafted design and meticulous preservation over the years. There are also other Tulou well-known for their very special shapes, such as stilt dwellings and mansion buildings.

■ 和贵楼

和贵楼建于清代1732年，坐西朝东，占地面积1,547平方米，建筑面积3,574平方米。楼始建为4层，1864年被盗匪烧毁，重建时加高为5层（前楼高17.08米，后楼高17.95米），成为列为世界文化遗产的福建土楼中"最高的方楼"。

和贵楼建在方圆3,000多平方米的沼泽地上，曾经用200多根直径20厘米的松木打桩、铺垫，历经200多年仍坚固稳定，巍然屹立。楼内共有140个房间，楼正中开一处大门，东西南北四方各有楼梯上下。由于该楼建在沼泽地上，游客在楼中的小天井里跺跺脚，就能感受到天井中整片鹅卵石的微微震动。楼中两口水井，井水水位均高出天井的地面，其中左边的井水清澈甘甜，另外一边的井水却不能饮用，两口水井相距不远，水质却截然相反，这也是该楼的一大奇观。该楼楼内还建有一个大约100多平方米的私塾学堂，旧时专门聘请名师宿儒教授土楼里面的男女学子，反映了和贵楼祖辈崇文重教、教育后代奋发向上的希冀。

和贵楼由楼和厝组成，大楼内围合厅堂天井的门厅和回廊即为"厝"，门外由单层平房（也为"厝"）围合成一个11米深的前院，正应了当地的俗语："厝包楼儿孙贤，楼包厝儿孙富。"

◎ 建在沼泽地上的土楼。（胡家新 摄）
Heguilou built on marshland. (Photo by Hu Jiaxin)

■ Heguilou

Heguilou was built during the Qing Dynasty around 1732. It sits in the west and faces the east. The land area is 1,547 square metres while the building area is 3,574 square metres. It is five storeys high (the front part stands 17.08 metres high while the back end is 17.95 metres high) and is the tallest square Tulou listed on the UNESCO World Heritage List.

◎ 神奇的鹅卵石地面。（冯木波 摄）
Magical pebbled patio. (Photo by Feng Mubo)

Heguilou was built on a 3,000-square metre marshland. It used to be dotted with more than 200 pine trees with a diameter of almost 20 centimetres which have remained firm and stable for more than 200 years. There are 140 rooms in the building, an entrance in the middle and a staircase in the east, west, north and south side of the Tulou. Because Heguilou was built on marshland, you can feel the vibrations rumbling through the stones if you stamp your feet in the pebbled patio. The water level in the building's two wells is higher than the level of the patio. The well on the left has clear drinking water while on the right, it would not be advisable to do as such. The two wells are not too far apart yet the water quality differs significantly, a rather peculiar aspect of this Tulou. A private school has also been set up. It takes up around 100 square metres of area. In the past, famous teachers were employed to teach the children living in the building.

■ 怀远楼

怀远楼是一座建于1905至1909年的双环圆形土楼，占地面积1,384.7平方米，建筑面积3,468平方米，外环楼高4层，每层34个房间，楼内有4部楼梯，1口水井。楼基以巨型鹅卵石和三合土垒筑，楼墙至今光整坚固，被视为古代生土夯筑技术研究的代表佳作。

怀远楼坐北朝南，楼的后面是林木茂密的大山。走进怀远楼大门可见一圆形天井。内院有一座"四架三间"的学堂，堂上悬挂一块刻着"斯是室"大字的横匾，是家族子弟读书的地方。"斯是室"设计考究，雕梁画栋，古色古香；堂中挂有几幅文雅秀气的对联。整个学堂充满了书香气息，充分彰显了楼主人读书报国平天下的抱负，凸显了土楼人家"耕读传家"的中国古代儒家思想。

楼内一至四层设有敞开回廊，采光充足，空气流通。楼顶屋檐下设有4个瞭望台，留有许多射击口，楼门正上方还设有3个防火灌水道。旧时如遇土匪强盗骚扰，楼内既有防火"装置"，又有可攻可守的瞭望台和射击口，整座土楼可保太平。正是有了这些独特的防御功能，怀远楼显得更加威严和神秘。

◎ 怀远楼雨后。（王福平 摄）

Huaiyuanlou after rain. (Photo by Wang Fuping)

◎ 怀远楼天井。（冯木波 摄）
The courtyard of Huaiyuanlou. (Photo by Feng Mubo)

■ Huaiyuanlou

The building structure of Huaiyuanlou consists of one circle within another and was built between 1905 and 1909. It covers a land area of 1,384.7 square metres and the building takes up an area of 3,468 square metres as a whole. The outer ring is four storeys high with 34 rooms per floor. There are four staircases and one well. The thick base is built with giant stones and reinforced with earth. The walls still have a smooth surface. It is regarded as the standard object for ancient earth architecture technology research.

Huaiyuanlou sits facing the south, and has a backdrop of green and lush mountains. Walking into Huaiyuanlou, there is a round patio. A hall split into three classrooms can be found in the inner courtyard with a plaque on the wall inscribed with the characters "斯是室" indicating that these are for learning purposes. The architecture of these rooms is quite lovely with vivid carvings and paintings. Several couplets can also be found hanging around the hall. This educational hall has a scholarly vibe and reflects the wishes of the residents to serve the country through learning.

Standing outside Huaiyuanlou, looking upwards, you can see there are four outlooks and many embrasures. There are also three fire prevention channels. Fire-proof mechanisms and shooting ports can also be found in the building – these were integrated in the old days to defend against any bandit attacks. It is with these defence measures that kept the peace at Huaiyuanlou, making it more majestic and mysterious.

◎ 怀远楼夜色。（冯木波 摄）
Night views. (Photo by Feng Mubo)

The first to fourth floors are open cloisters, allowing plenty of light and air circulation. A few small windows are on the fourth for defensive purposes and on the outer wall, there are four observation platforms facing all four directions. Three water tanks are buried in the railing over the gate. All these strengthen the building's defensive function.

◎ 荷塘映土楼。（冯木波 摄）
The lotus pond in front of the Tulou. (Photo by Feng Mubo)

华安大地土楼群

华安大地土楼群位于福建省漳州市华安县仙都镇大地村，距离华安县城26千米。大地村三面环山，两条小溪穿村而过，串起数十座土楼。其中二宜楼、南阳楼、东阳楼三座土楼是世界文化遗产"福建土楼"的组成部分。三座土楼为蒋氏祖孙在清朝时期所建，距今有200多年历史，其独具特色的建筑平面布局、防卫功能、构造处理、建筑装饰以及每座土楼的石制匾额上刻有的建造年代，都让大地土楼群显得与众不同。

Dadi Tulou Cluster in Hua'an

Dadi Tulou Cluster can be found in Dadi Village in Hua'an County, Zhangzhou, 26 kilometres away from the county town. Dozens of Tulou are located along the two streams running through the village, among which three Tulou are listed as the World Heritage sites. These three Tulou are Eryilou, Nanyanglou and Dongyanglou. These were built by the Jiang ancestors during Emperor Kangxi's reign in the Qing Dynasty. They have witnessed more than 200 years of history and have unique architectural layouts, defensive functions, construction processes, interior design and each Tulou has the year they were built engraved on a plaque. These are the special characteristics that make Hua'an Tulou Cluster unique today.

◎ 大地土楼群。（胡家新 摄）
Dadi Tulou Cluster. (Photo by Hu Jiaxin)

◎ "土楼之王"二宜楼。（王福平 摄）
A King of Tulou. (Photo by Wang Fuping)

■ 二宜楼

二宜楼坐落于大地村的中部，是一座建于清乾隆五年（1740）的双环圆形土楼，坐东南朝西北，占地面积9,300平方米，外环高4层，内环单层。整座土楼分为16个单元，除了4个单元是公用的梯道及厅堂等，其余12个单元均为相对独立的住户。与其他内通廊式土楼相比，更具有居家私密性。内环的平房作为厨房和饭厅；外环的底层为客厅，二、三层为卧室，四层为各家祖堂，两个侧室为粮仓。楼内有一个大门和两个边门，楼中心是一个占地约600平方米的大院子，设有2口水井。

二宜楼外墙厚达2.53米，墙脚石砌、墙身夯土。底层外墙体有12个"之"字形传声洞，二层以上墙厚慢慢减薄，顶层设1米宽的环形外圈的"隐通廊"，将全楼连通。外圈通廊与4层的祖堂之间有小门相通，设观察窗和射击窗56个，枪眼23个。楼层内圈也设走廊，单元之间有门洞相通。门开启，全楼内圈走廊可以环行；门关闭，则各单元自成一体。二宜楼的这种利用传声洞、泄沙漏水孔、秘密地下通道、隐通廊等构成的防卫系统，构思独到，堪称古代战略防御与民居生活完美结合的典范。

◎ 欢庆二宜楼。（胡家新 摄）

Celebration in Eryilou. (Photo by Hu Jiaxin)

■ Eryilou

Located in the middle of Dadi Village, Eryilou is a double-ring Tulou built in 1740. It sits in the southeast and faces northwest. Taking up a land area of 9,300 square metres, the outer ring has four floors while the inner ring is a single layer. The whole building is divided into 16 units. Four of the units have shared stairways and halls while the remaining 12 units are households with separate stairways. In comparison with other Tulou that have an inner corridor, this is more intimate as a home. The inner ring serves as the kitchen and dining room. The lower floor of the outer ring is the living room, and the second and third floor are full of bedrooms and the fourth floor is the ancestral hall with two side rooms as granaries. There is a main gate and two side entrances. The inner courtyard is an area of 600 square metres for all residents and features two wells.

The outer wall of Eryilou is 2.53 metres thick, the base made of stone and the wall itself made of earth. On the ground floor, the outer wall has 12 zigzag sound holes. The thickness of the walls from the second floor upwards are slightly thinner. The top floor was designed with a one metre wide corridor that connects the entire floor. There is a small door between the outer circle corridor and the ancestral hall on the top floor. It provides peripheral observation with 56 small windows to shoot arrows from, and 23 embrasures like openings for guns. There is also a corridor in the inner circle and doors that connect each of the units. When the doors are opened, the inner corridor of the whole building can be looped. When the doors are closed, the units are self-contained. The kind of defensive measures Eryilou was designed with, such as sound holes and secret underground passages, is a model of the perfect combination of the ancient strategic defence and ancient folk life.

　　走进二宜楼，处处让人感受到古朴雄浑、幽深宁静。成百上千处丰富多彩、寓意深远的彩绘、壁画、楹联、木雕，内容有山水、花鸟、人物等，文化内涵十分丰富厚重，是一座罕见的民间艺术宝库。除了这些民间艺术珍品，二宜楼的墙上和天花板上还张贴着1931年的美国《布鲁克林日报》和1932年的美国《纽约晚报》，墙上还绘有西洋钟、西洋美女并标注译文的壁画，让人惊讶之余，感受到这座土楼里中西方文化的碰撞。二宜楼规模宏大、设计科学，耗时30年方得以建成，又有历史悠久、文化厚重、保存完好等几大特点，成就了"土楼之王"的美誉。

◎ 西式壁画。（胡家新 摄）
Murals of western style.
(Photo by Hu Jiaxin)

◎ 1931年的《布鲁克林日报》。
（王福平 摄）
Brocklyn Daily dated 1931.
(Photo by Wang Fuping)

When you walk into Eryilou, there is a wave of tranquility and simplicity. Hundreds of colourful paintings, meaningful murals, couplets and wood carvings can be found everywhere. The contents of these arts are rich landscapes, flowers, birds and figures. Eryilou is a treasure of folk art, rich with cultural connotations. The interior of Eryilou is a wonderful display of Western and Chinese culture coming together. On the ceilings, you can find pages from America's *Brocklyn Daily* dated 1931 and *New York Evening News* dated 1932. Turn your attention to the walls and you will find painted murals of Western style clockworks and American ladies. Eryilou, which took 30 years to be constructed, has a reputation for being a Tulou king due to its long history, grand scale, abundant culture and well-preserved features.

◎ 祖先供堂的壁画。（王福平 摄）
Colored murals in the hall. (Photo by Wang Fuping)

◎ 倒影入清漪。（冯木波 摄）
Nanyanglou and its reflection. (Photo by Feng Mubo)

■ 南阳楼

　　南阳楼位于二宜楼东南侧，两楼相距约150米，是一座建于清嘉庆二十二年（1817）的双环圆形土楼，坐东南朝西北，占地面积3,100平方米，外环高3层13.25米，内环单层。

　　南阳楼是以二宜楼为蓝本修建的，充分吸收了二宜楼建筑设计方面的特点，同样拥有传声洞、泄沙漏水孔、秘密地下通道、隐通廊等防卫系统，其使用的木雕、石刻等材料又比二宜楼更优。而且石刻雕工特别精致，尤其是祖堂前的抱鼓石，不大的表面竟雕刻有数十种吉兽神禽。除此之外，南阳楼还有一个特色就是站在天井中心在两米范围内有明显的回音共鸣效果，这在福建世遗土楼中也是比较罕见的。

■ Nanyanglou

Nanyanglou is located on the southeast side of Eryilou. The distance between the two Tulou is about 150 metres. Nanyanglou is also a double-ringed Tulou built in 1817. Facing the northwest, it covers an area of 3,100 square metres. The outer ring is 3 storeys high at 13.25 metres. The inner ring is a single floor.

Nanyanglou was built based on Eryilou and thus shares some similarities in terms of architectural design such as the sound holes, the secret underground passage and defence mechanisms. The difference is that the materials used here are possibly better than Eryilou. The stone carvings are carefully crafted, particularly the drum shaped stone located at the front of the ancestral hall and the many legendary beasts engraved on the sides. Another special aspect of Nanyanglou is that within two metres of the centre of the patio, there is an echo resonance effect, a rare attribute among Fujian Tulou.

◎ 最宜居的东阳楼。（冯木波 摄）
The most liveable Tulou. (Photo by Feng Mubo)

■ 东阳楼

东阳楼位于南阳楼西侧，是一座建于清嘉庆二十二年（1817）的方形土楼，遗留着从五凤楼演变到方形土楼的痕迹。该楼坐西北朝东南，占地面积2,200平方米。主楼高2层11米，有住房36间，厅4个，主楼两边各建有15间平房。

东阳楼内整个建筑前低后高，错落有致。其最大的特色是单元式布局和内通廊式建筑风格的完美结合，建筑设计由防御为主向追求舒适转变，这是福建土楼建筑的一大突破，因此东阳楼也被称为"最宜居的土楼"，现在仍有13个家庭近50人在这里居住。

东阳楼和南阳楼都背靠狮子山，山清水秀，绿竹成荫，风光秀丽，两座土楼一方一圆，阴阳相济，天圆地方，与周围的自然景观交相辉映、浑然一体,独具闽南田园风光的特色。

■ Dongyanglou

To the west of Nanyanglou is Dongyanglou. It is a square Tulou built in 1817. There are traces of the evolution from the pavilion style Tulou to the square shape. Facing the southeast, Dongyanglou covers an area of 2,200 square metres. At most, the building has two levels standing at 11 metres high, with the main part of the Tulou having 36 rooms, and four halls. On either side of the main section are two lower areas that contain 15 rooms.

The entire building has a low front high back structure. It paid much attention to comfort of living instead of being defence oriented as other Tulou built before. This was a major breakthrough in Fujian Tulou construction and therefore, Dongyanglou is known as the most liveable Tulou. Now around 50 residents from 13 families live together in this Tulou.

Both Dongyanglou and Nanyanglou are situated in front of Lion Rock. The scenery is worth taking a few moments to appreciate with one square and one circular Tulou sitting amongst the green bamboo and flowing bodies of water, a complementing combination of natural landscapes and human creation.

其他著名土楼

　　福建土楼成千上万，穿行于闽西南的山山水水，不经意间，一座座土楼就会从你身边掠过。除了列为世界文化遗产的46座福建土楼，还有很多很多的土楼值得你去发现。

Other Famous Tulou

Thousands of Tulou are situated amongst the mountains and the rivers of southwest Fujian and as such, inadvertently, you may happen upon many of these earthen buildings. In addition to the 46 Fujian Tulou listed on the UNESCO World Cultural Heritage List, there are many others worthy of discovery.

◎ 青山掩土楼。（冯木波 摄）
The Tulou among mountains. (Photo by Feng Mubo)

■ 环极楼

环极楼位于永定湖坑镇南中村，因为楼中心的回音效果和抗震性能强而出名，吸引了不少游客前来参观。站在该楼天井正中的圆心处用力跺脚、呼喊、唱歌，能听见清晰的回音，离开中心点以后，回声立刻消失。另外，该楼抗震性能极强，历经多次地震仍稳如泰山，其中一次地震过后，墙体裂缝，却奇迹般慢慢合拢，仅留下一条细长的裂痕。

■ Huanjilou

Huanjilou, located at Nanzhong Village of Yongding, is famous for its echo and strong seismic performance at the centre of the building, thus attracting many visitors throughout the year. Standing at the centre, any sounds of screaming, shouting or singing will create a clear echo but it disappears immediately you move away from the centre. Huanjilou has witnessed many earthquakes, but has stood its ground, even when there are cracks as a result of the natural disaster. These cracks will miraculously close together leaving only a sliver in the wall.

◎ 闪电惊醒环极楼。（胡家新 摄）
Lightning over Huanjilou. (Photo by Hu Jiaxin)

◎ 永康楼内精美的屏风。（胡家新 摄）
The luxuriant screen in Yongkanglou. (Photo by Hu Jiaxin)

■ 永康楼

　　位于永定区下洋镇霞村的永康楼是一座通廊式圆形土楼，内院布局考究，建筑装饰精美，前厅檐下的彩绘中有洋房、大桥、飞机、火车、轮船等近现代景观，门扇雕刻的戏曲人物惟妙惟肖，展现了福建土楼中不多见的富丽堂皇，被视为最华丽的圆形土楼之一。

■ Yongkanglou

Yongkanglou is located in Xia Village, Xiayang Town of Yongding District. It is a corridor-style circular Tulou. The architectural and interior design of the inner courtyard is exquisite. Paintings of modern landscapes such as houses, bridges, planes, trains and ships hang in the front hall while opera figures have been vividly carved into the sides of the door. Its artistry has made it one of the most magnificent Fujian Tulou to visit.

◎ 精妙的空间布局。（胡家新 摄）

The spacious layout. (Photo by Hu Jiaxin)

■ 遗经楼

位于永定区高陂镇上洋村的遗经楼占地面积约为1.13万平方米，规模宏大、坚实牢固。该楼前楼4层，后楼5层，主楼左右为2层的护门楼，楼内共有328间房间、24个厅堂、2个穿堂、4座学堂、2座花园等。整座土楼是单元式方楼和内通廊式方楼的结合，这在福建方楼中是少有的。因此该楼以空间布局精妙、艺术格调高雅、建筑气势宏伟等特色，被视为最为壮观的方形土楼之一。

■ Yijinglou

Located in Shangyang Village, Gaobei Town of Yongding District, Yijinglou covers an area of about 11,300 square metres, a large and solid structure. The front of the building stands four storeys high, the back building five storeys high and on both sides of the main building stand two-storey gatehouses. There are 328 rooms, 24 halls, 2 side halls, 4 schools and 2 gardens just to name a few sections that can be found in Yijinglou. The entire Tulou structure is a combination of a modular building and an inner gallery, a rare design amongst the Fujian Tulou. Because of this, it has a spacious layout, composing of elegant artistic styles as well as architectural styles, making it the most spectacular square Tulou to see.

■ 南靖裕昌楼

　　位于南靖县书洋镇下坂村的裕昌楼始建于1308至1338年，该楼外环为五层楼，是南靖土楼楼层最多、楼高最高的圆形土楼。该楼由5个姓氏的家族共同建造，5个姓氏，5层楼，不知是巧合还是有意为之。

　　此楼最神奇之处是看起来整座土楼摇摇欲坠，最大倾斜度达15度，但是，历经700年风雨侵蚀和无数次地震以后，依旧巍然屹立，有惊无险，所以裕昌楼又称"东倒西歪楼"，现改为"东歪西斜楼"，被誉为"中华第一奇楼"。

■ Yuchanglou in Nanjing

Yuchanglou is located in Xiaban Village, Shuyang Town in Nanjing County. It was built between 1308 and 1338. The outer ring of the Tulou is five storeys high and it is the largest Tulou with the highest floor height as well as building height in Nanjing. This Tulou was built by five different families. It is not certain whether the five floors and five families is a coincidence or intentional.

The most amazing aspect about Yuchanglou is that the entire building looks like it may be crumbling due to a maximum inclination of 15 degrees. However, after 700 years of weathering and withstanding countless earthquakes, it holds its ground proudly and resiliently. Yuchanglou is often known as China's most mysterious building.

◎ "东歪西斜楼"的星光。（冯木波 摄）
The star light over Yuchanglou. (Photo by Feng Mubo)

■ 翠林楼

翠林楼位于南靖县南坑镇新罗村，建于清嘉庆年间（1796—1820），是世界上最小的圆形土楼，楼高不足8米，内径仅9米，周长不足30米，相当袖珍。该楼因镶嵌在翠谷绿林间而得其名。

■ Cuilinlou

Cuilinlou is located in Xinluo Village, Nankeng Town of Nanjing County in Zhangzhou. It was built in the Qing Dynasty during Emperor Jiaqing's reign (1796—1820). It is the smallest circular Tulou in the world with a height of less than 8 metres, an inner diameter of 9 metres and a circumference less than 30 metres. It is quite compact and is named after its location in the green valley.

◎ 福建最小的土楼。（胡家新 摄）
The smallest Tulou in Fujian. (Photo by Hu Jiaxin)

◎ 绳武楼。（冯木波 摄）
Shengwulou. ((Photo by Feng Mubo)

■ 绳武楼

　　位于漳州市平和县芦溪镇焦路村的绳武楼始建于清朝嘉庆年间，历经4代100多年终于建成。楼内处处可见石雕、木雕、泥塑、壁画、彩绘等，其中完整地保留了建楼时的精细木雕近700处，数量之多，无一雷同，雕工精致，精美绝伦，有专家称之为"木雕博物馆"。

■ Shengwulou

Shengwulou is located in Jiaolu Village, Luxi Town in Pinghe County of Zhangzhou. Construction started in the Qing Dynasty during Emperor Jiaqing's reign but was not completed until over a century later. Within the building, there are stone and wood carvings, clay sculptures and mural paintings. Nearly 700 of the wood carvings have existed since the Tulou had begun to be built. Each is unique and with fine and intricate carving techniques. Some would even say Shengwulou is much like a wood sculpture museum.

◎ 精美的木雕。（冯木波 摄）
Wood carvings. (Photo by Feng Mubo)

◎ 三眼井。（冯木波 摄）

The three-hole well. (Photo by Feng Mubo)

■ 阙宁楼

　　阙宁楼坐落于漳州市平和县芦溪镇，始建于清康熙年间，历时40年才完工。该楼每一扇门里面有四层楼和独立的院子，空间相对独立，这种设计的土楼，在福建土楼来说是罕见的。楼内中庭宽敞，水井由三个洞组成，是一口极具特色的三眼井。据考证，该楼是目前已知最早登上邮票（英国明信片）的土楼。

■ Queninglou

Queninglou is located in Luxi Town, Pinghe County in Zhangzhou. It was built in the Qing Dynasty during Emperor Kangxi's reign and took 40 years to complete. There are four floors and an independent yard. The different sections of the Tulou are relatively independent. The front hall in the building is spacious and there is a three-hole well. This sort of design is rare for Fujian Tulou. It was said Queninglou was the first to be printed on English postcards.

土楼家园——聚族而居的田园生活

　　走进土楼，走进土楼人家的日常生活，你会被土楼人家的仁慈敦厚、团结友爱、和善睦邻、热情好客的淳朴民风所深深陶醉。

　　一座土楼就是一个家族，里面少则十几户人家，多则几十户。家家户户血缘相近、同宗共祖，大家长幼有序，团结互助。每一座土楼都遵循着祖祖辈辈流传下来的生活规矩，过着平淡而又令人向往的田园牧歌式的生活。土楼人家共有天井、厅堂等公共场所，共用石磨、谷砻、石舂、水井、谷风车等公共物品。

◎ 宁静的土楼田园生活。（陈军 摄）
A life in peace and rusticity. (Photo by Chen Jun)

Tulou Courtyard : A Day in the Life of a Small Tulou

Upon entering a Tulou, you will always be greeted by an overwhelming warmth. Being kind, enthusiastic and friendly, the Tulou people are truly hospitable.

Each Tulou houses a clan, ranging from a dozen families to dozens of families. Most families share ancestors generations back, contributing to a strong sense of community. Each Tulou has its own way of living, having been passed down from generation to generation, leading peaceful and idyllic lives. Enjoying a communal living, the Tulou people share public spaces and resources such as halls, grain hullers, wells, winnowers and mills.

热情好客的土楼人家

　　土楼居民几乎家家户户夜不闭户，平时也只用两扇矮小的木栅门拦着，这是防鸡鸭跑进屋的。谁家的老人或者小孩饿了，只要谁家锅里有吃的，都可以自行进去食用。谁家有红白喜事，楼里面马上会启动"理事会"，选出主事的人，全楼的人都主动前来帮忙，按照理事会的安排，井井有条地把事情做好。楼内谁家遇到困难了，大家就有钱出钱、有力出力，齐心协力共渡难关。楼内谁家杀了猪，主人就先用猪血和猪大肠煮酸菜，一碗一碗地送给左邻右舍，卖剩下的猪肉再每户一份地送到邻居家里，与族人一同分享收获的喜悦。楼内每逢春节或者重大的节日、民俗活动、公益活动等，大家都会群策群力，善始善终。如果遇到冬季阴冷的日子，有时候土楼内会生起篝火，请来乡间艺人，大家和着竹板敲出的节拍，唱着客家山歌、跳起客家舞蹈，其乐融融……

　　不管你来自哪里，不管你要去哪一村哪一家，只要你随便走进一户人家，土楼的主人都会热情地接待你：一杯冒着香气的热茶，一根自制的香烟，一盘当地盛产的水果。闲聊片刻，若要问路，土楼人家便会仔仔细细教你怎么走，路途较远的话，他们会干脆直接骑着摩托车把你载到要去的地方。如果恰逢节假日，主人们早早就把平时都舍不得吃的鸡鸭鱼肉准备好了，还有一壶壶精心酿制的米酒。不管是土楼里哪一户人家来了客人，都会成为这整座土楼的贵客，各家各户端出自家最好的酒菜，向客人敬酒，让客人尽兴而归。

◎ 热闹的厨房。（张耀辉 摄）
Busy kitchen. (Photo by Zhang Yaohui)

◎ 美食待客。（张耀辉 摄）

Making special food for guests. (Photo by Zhang Yaohui)

A Warm and Welcoming Family Home

Most nights, doors are left unlocked, and during the day, the doors on the first floor are blocked only with low wooden fencing to prevent animals from running in and out. If anyone goes hungry, anyone with food will offer him a bite to eat. If any family slaughters a pig, they will cook and share a large meal with their neighbours, and parcel out any unsold pork. If anyone is struggling, the community will do their best to support them, overcoming the difficulties as one. The whole community comes together for major affairs, such as weddings or the passing of family members, carrying them out with respect and pride. During every major festival, such as the Chinese Spring Festival, families will celebrate together, doing some community service and carrying on traditions. Some cold winter days, a bonfire will be lit in the courtyard of the Tulou, where people will gather to sing folk music, dance and enjoy their time together.

Regardless of where you are from or where you are going, the Tulou people will welcome you into their midst with a hot cup of tea, a homemade cigarette and some fruit. After some chat, they will be more than happy to point you in the right direction. If you're looking to travel far, they may even take you there via motorcycle. If you happen to be there on a holiday, you could be offered some of the precious duck or fish they'd been saving for the occasion, with some rice wine on the side. No matter which family you may be there for, you are an important guest of the whole Tulou, and they will treat you as such so that you return home with content.

诗情画意的土楼清晨

一阵嘹亮的鸡鸣声此起彼伏，一缕清新透明的空气扑面而来，然后，一个古老的村庄一群沧桑的土楼便真真实实原原本本地呈现在你的眼前。略带些凉意的早晨，居住在土楼的村民早早起床了。家庭主妇们房前屋后巡视一番，一会儿喊住路过卖肉的小贩，一会儿去自家菜园摘几棵葱几根大蒜，赶回家烧火做饭。不一会儿工夫，一盆盆喷香的饭菜、一大碗冒着热气的瘦肉猪肝粉肠汤就摆在饭桌上了，让家里已经干完农活的男人以及刚刚睡醒的孩子们垂涎欲滴。

一位老者，整整衣裳，清清嗓子，捋了捋袖子，打开家里的鸡舍鸭舍，一边用只有这些鸡鸭才听得懂的话唤着，一边从碗中抓出一把米饭或是稻谷向它们撒去。山的那一边飘来阵阵铿锵有力的客家山歌，一位光着膀子的中年大叔正远远地从山那一头的田间小路上走来，肩上扛着一捆干柴和竹子，他一边唱着客家山歌一边用毛巾擦着汗水，在清晨霞光的照射下，还能隐隐约约看到他那黝黑的皮肤上挂着点点汗珠。大叔山歌唱完唱情歌，羞得那小溪边洗衣服的客家媳妇低下了头，一边扬起棒槌拍打衣服，一边在清清的河水中来回搓洗着。

土楼的清晨生活连同那低飞的小鸟清脆悦耳的鸟鸣声，划过村庄的山山水水，划过或方或圆的瓦楞，划过慢慢升起的朝霞和炊烟，就这样如诗如画般开启新的一天。

◎ 早起的土楼人。（王福平 摄）
Early birds of the Tulou. (Photo by Wang Fuping)

The Picturesque Morning

To the sounds chirping of birds, the feel of crisp air, and in all its magnificence, a proud Tulou village wakes up in the morning. The residents have been awake since dawn. Housewives busy themselves harvesting food from their own vegetable garden and buying other ingredients. They go home and prepare a meal, so that when the men finish working in the field and the children wake up, there is a rich breakfast of vegetables, rice and a steaming hot bowl of pork liver soup on the table.

An elderly man, dressed impeccably, clears his throat, dusts off his sleeves and opens the chicken coop. In a soothing voice, he coaxes the animals towards him as he sprinkles the ground with grain.

From the mountain drifts a Hakka folk song, as a lone, shirtless man returns carrying firewood and bamboo. As he continues singing the song, he wipes away the sweat on his brow, and under the bright sun, glistening sweat can be seen on his dark skin. As he finishes his song, the women nearby return to their chore, washing clothes in the river.

As all this happens, the early birds fly by, singing their song. They fly past the great Tulou, the mountains, the brooks and the field. It is in this setting that a new day starts at the Tulou.

◎ 南江村之晨。（陈军 摄）
Morning of Nanjiang Village. (Photo by Chen Jun)

惬意悠然的中午时分

土楼人一天中最惬意的时光当属中午了。土楼里响起锅碗瓢盆声、切菜烧菜声、孩童欢笑声、大人交谈声，土楼里面顿时热闹了起来。一阵功夫，午饭做好了，土楼居民盛好饭菜，三三两两串起门来，你尝我家的菜，我喝你家的汤，大家一边吃还一边夸，议论着谁的手艺最好。

更多的土楼居民端着饭菜，聚集到土楼门口，坐在被数百年风雨磨光的石板凳上，或一条条陈年旧板凳上。他们一边吃着饭，一边聊着家常，说说谁家的媳妇生孩子啦，谁家的孩子考上什么大学啦，总是有聊不完的话题。小狗也来凑热闹，在人们脚边讨着食物。这些石板凳和旧板凳见证了土楼几代人甚至十几代人老老少少在这里吃饭、纳凉、闲聊的热闹温馨的场景，见证了土楼风雨几百年的岁月变迁。

◎ 总有说不完的话。（赖永生 摄）
Talking about the going-ons. (Photo by Lai Yongsheng)

午饭以后，热闹了一阵的土楼开始安静下来。劳累了大半天的村民们有的回房间睡午觉，有的叼根烟，围着土楼这边走走、那边看看，有的则细心地整理下午要使用的农具。如果是烈日炎炎的夏天，老人和孩子们便会在土楼里面的板凳上或躺或坐，因为土楼冬暖夏凉的缘故，特别是靠近大门的地方格外凉爽，这里的板凳成了纳凉的好地方。土楼的墙角边或者院子里的阴凉处，看家的小狗吐着舌头喘着粗气，成群的鸡鸭懒洋洋地躲在柴火后面或者树荫下面。这个时候，在习以为常的蝉鸣声中，夏日的土楼午后显得那么安静、那么悠然。

◎ 吃百家饭的土楼孩子。（赖永生 摄）
Sharing food. (Photo by Lai Yongsheng)

The Lazy Midday

For the residents of the Tulou, midday is the best part of the day. The whole building comes alive with the noise of pots and pans, the chopping of vegetables, the laughter of children and the sounds of conversation. As families come together to enjoy lunch, they share with each other their own food, and over the din of the meal, praises are hurled back and forth, each claiming someone else to be an amazing cook.

People also gather at the entrance to the Tulou, sitting on humble wooden seats or stone benches polished by centuries of rain. As they eat, they talk about the going-ons of life – where their sons and daughters are studying, whether or not they're having children, and other idle chatter. Pets also join in the fray, frolicking in the near vicinity. These benches have witnessed generations of this community, as the Tulou community lounge about at noon, growing their relationships.

After lunch, the atmosphere settles down. People head in different directions to take naps, smoke a cigarette, take a walk, or prepare themselves for the afternoon work ahead. In the hot summer sun, the elderly and the young will hideaway inside, as the interior of the Tulou is cool during summer and warm during winter. In nooks, crannies and patches of shade, puppies pant and rest after their adventures, while the ducks and chickens also look for a place to shelter. It is a wave of quiet peacefulness that takes over the Tulou, interrupted only by the singing of cicadas.

欢乐祥和的土楼之夜

傍晚时分，夜幕缓缓垂下来。土楼村里的山前山后，屋前屋后，家家户户的炊烟慢慢升起。大人们房前屋后地忙着，有的抱柴做饭，有的吆喝着把白天放养出去的鸡鸭鹅赶回鸡舍鸭舍里。放学归来的孩子们有的复习功课，有的朗诵客家三字经，有的玩捉迷藏，一会儿躲在墙角旁，一会儿躲在大人的身后，一会儿躲在楼梯下；孩子们自己制作了各种玩具，玩滚铁环、打陀螺、跳格子、跳绳、踢毽子等游戏。偌大的土楼里，孩子的欢笑声、呼喊声此起彼伏，整座土楼成了孩子们的天地。

夜色下的晚餐，格外有客家韵味。一声声用客家话猜拳的声音传来，原来是村民们在一起喝着自家酿制的米酒，就着农村自家养的鸡鸭鱼肉，以及那闻着就流口水的客家酸菜、爆炒过后香气四溢的花生米。他们时而满脸通红青筋暴涨，时而满脸笑容，时而端起一碗米酒一饮而尽，时而夹着一筷子菜擦擦嘴巴。他们的猜拳声在宁静的小山村显得尤其豪放，喝到尽兴的时候，大家开始唱起山歌，你一首我一曲，土楼这头唱着，土楼的那头和着。

喝完酒吃完饭，土楼居民们便会把碗筷收掉，把喝酒改为喝茶了。茶叶自然也是靠着辛勤的双手采摘制作的。土楼里的制茶技术也是传承了祖祖辈辈的制茶手艺，基本上每家每户都会制作茶叶。土楼居民喝茶自然也是跟喝酒一样，你一杯，我一杯。喝茶的时候，大家把平日里的苦平日里的累，以及平日里无法言语的心里话都说出来，互相倾诉，互相安慰。你一言我一语，坦诚直爽，没有假情假意。

夜深人静的时候，土楼里某个房间只要声音大一些，相邻的房间都能听见；而且房间朝向楼道的窗户开得很低，但土楼人似乎并不在乎这些。他们彼此息息相通、坦坦荡荡、亲密无间，内心是那样豁达、纯朴、善良。

◎ 整个土楼就是孩子们的天地。（胡家新 摄）
The Tulou belongs to the children at this moment. (Photo by Hu Jiaxin)

The Tranquil Night

Night falls slowly, as afternoon transitions to evening, and slowly, one by one, smoke rises from the chimneys of each building. The adults hustle and bustle, some cooking, some tending to the fire, and others herding the chickens. The children are busy doing their homework, learning Hakka stories, or entertaining themselves – be that hide and seek, jumping rope, whipping tops or rolling iron hoops. In this vast Tulou, the laughter and joyful cries of children float through the air, and for a while, the Tulou belongs to the children.

Dinner carries distinctly Hakka flavours, a result of recipes handed down through the generations. Shouts in the local dialect when playing drinking games can be heard, as the villagers relax over a casual rice wine, with accompanying snacks such as self-produced meats, preserved vegetables and seasoned peanuts. Flushed red, their faces are filled with excitement as they settle into the night. Their boisterous voices and laughter carry on the wind, and they even break out in song, filling the Tulou with delight from one end to the other.

As dinner comes to an end, the dishes are packed away, and in the place of wine is tea. The tea, of course, is locally harvested too. At the Tulou, tea making techniques have also been passed down through generations, and practically everyone household know how to preserve their tea leaves and prepare tea. Much like with alcohol, residents share a cup of tea whilst spending time together. In contrast to the high-spirited conversation over alcohol, however, people tend to be more reflective and thoughtful over tea. The otherwise unspoken feelings and tiredness reveal themselves at this time, and the people listen to and comfort one another. It is an honest and kind exchange, with a deep sense of trust.

Deep into the night, noise travels easily in the Tulou. Even a little noise can be heard by the neighbours, and despite the windows facing the corridors being very low, the Tulou people don't seem to care. They truly are a close, intimate, kind and open community.

○ 土楼夜色。（王福平 摄）
Beautiful sight on a full moon night (Photo by Wang Fuping)

古老土地上的春耕美景

"布谷飞飞劝早耕，春锄扑扑趁春晴。千层石树遥行路，一带山田放水声。"这是清代著名散文家姚鼐的诗词《山行》，诗中描绘了一幅繁忙热闹的春耕图。而这也正是土楼春耕的写照。

土楼的先民开山造田，从山脚到山顶，只要有一点空地，都能开垦出一块田地。于是沿着山坡开垦出来的一垄垄稻田便成了排列整齐、美丽壮观的梯田。春雷阵阵，细雨蒙蒙。立春之后，勤劳的土楼人家就要开始为春耕做准备了，今年准备种多少地，便准备好多少种子，开始一年之中最重要的耕耘播种。

春耕讲求精耕细作，耕作分为"一犁二耙三压平"三个步骤。初春的早晨，农人们牵着牛、扛着犁和耙，早早来到田里。他们把牛轭往牛颈上一放，便开始犁田了。牛走在前面，牛轭上系着一根绳子，农人一手拉紧绳子，一手扶着犁，吆喝着牛往前走。牛一停一走，农人一高一低，默契地配合着，把田里的泥土深翻起来。每一垅田犁过以后，农人再把翻好的土耙过一遍，把泥土碾细、整平。接着还要人工再压平，让整垄田都能平整，便于播种。

田整好以后，农人开始把浸泡好的种子撒到田里育苗。从种子发芽到秧苗成长大概需要一个月左右的时间。到那时候，农户便开始根据天气情况，把要种的稻田再犁过一遍、耙过一遍，然后才开始一边拔秧苗，一边插秧。拔秧苗也是要讲究技巧的，农人们或蹲着或拿着一个小矮凳子坐着，把秧苗拔出来扎成一小撮。插秧之前，农人会把一小撮一小撮准备的秧苗均匀地往田里扔过去。这样便于插秧的人可以随时在身边拿到准备好的秧苗，不用在泥地里为了拿秧苗走来走去。

插秧的时候，农人们一般是先往横着的方向插上几根禾苗，有了这个第一排禾苗作为标记，大家便以接近八九十度的弯度弓着腰，一边往田里插着秧，一边往后退。每过几分钟便会直起腰，一来舒展一下腰身，二来看看前面插的秧有没有对齐，观察四周是否有一些禾苗没插好而浮在水面。

如果在没过膝盖的水田里插秧更要费力很多，一边要好不容易把脚从水田里拔出来，一边还要把秧深深地插进稻田里面，还要随时提防陷到泥里。如果碰到下雨天气，农人们还要披着用塑料薄膜做成的雨衣，戴着用棕叶做成的草帽，一边顶着三月的冷风细雨，一边还要用将近冻僵的手往田里插秧。雨若大些的时候，滴到田里的雨水还会溅到脸上甚至嘴巴上。

等一垄田插秧完以后，站在田埂上，一眼望去，一排排整整齐齐的禾苗昂起头颅，微风中向农人频频点头致意，表示感谢。此时，农人心中却总会油然而生一种满足感，似乎看到了收获的希望。

土楼人大多聚族而居，每到春耕时候，大家都会发扬互帮互助的传统美德，你一家，我一家，大家一边干活，一边有说有笑，使冷风中的春耕显得那么温情热闹。春耕前后，有的地方还会举办春耕节、"迎春牛"民俗及各种春耕祭祀活动。因为春耕时常烟雨蒙蒙，云雾缭绕在土楼四周，农人和牛在层层梯田上耕作，构成一幅十分美丽的春耕图，所以这个时节土楼的田野里总是聚集了无数的摄影爱好者。

◎ 土楼春耕。（王福平 摄）

Spring ploughing in the Tulou area. (Photo by Wang Fuping)

◎ 快乐春耕。（冯木波 摄）
A happy couple ploughing.
(Photo by Feng Mubo)

The Beautiful Approach of Spring

The poem "Walking in the Mountains" by Yao Nai describes the beautiful livelihood of farmers as spring approaches, and it is the exact scene that can be seen at the Tulou.

The first settlers built the Tulou and tilled the land, creating farmland up the side of the mountain. Over time, these have become picturesque terrace fields. As spring approaches, the weather changes, bringing the spring rain. The Tulou people set aside land and seeds, a crucial part of preparation for sowing for the next harvest.

Spring ploughing is an important process that marks the beginning of cultivation. Divided into three parts, this process involves ploughing, tilling and then flattening the land. In the mornings of early spring, farmers take oxen and yokes to plough the land. It is a process that requires cooperation between the oxen and the farmer but is one that has been mastered over time. After this, the ground is finely tilled. Finally, it is flattened so that it is easy to sow grain.

It is at this point that the farmers sow the prepared seeds into the fields. It takes about a month from the seeds germinating until sprouts can be seen popping out. At that time, the farmers will need to manage the fields and seedlings carefully. Transplanting seedlings is a delicate process that requires skill. Sitting on a small wooden stool, farmers carefully uproot the seedlings and bundle them up, taking care not to damage the roots. These seedling bundles are gathered together so that when it is time to put them back into the soil, they are ready.

Usually, a row of seedlings is planted first. From there, farmers will plant rice seedlings using the first row as a point of reference. Bent over, they move backwards one step at a time, planting as they go. Every so often, they will stand up straight to stretch a little, make sure they are still in line, and make sure the planted seedlings have stayed in the ground.

Working in the wet fields can be difficult. Not only do they have to plant the seedling carefully, it also takes significant effort to take steps as gumboots are very easily caught in the mud. Some days, the farmers wear raincoats and straw hats to ward off the cold March rain, but it can still soak them to the bone.

Each planted field is a sight to behold; row upon row of neatly planted seedlings. A light breeze wafts by, and the seedlings nod—as if to pay tribute to the farmers, who give off an immense sense of pride and satisfaction for a job well done, and hope for a bountiful harvest.

In this busy time, the community comes together as one. One family helps another family, and that family passes it on, until everyone is helping where they can. They tell jokes and converse, creating a warm environment in the bitter cold. Some Tulou even hold a festival to celebrate this spring planting with various customs including a ritual where a cow "welcomes spring". Additionally, photographers love to come at this time of year, when the whole valley is turned into a mesmerising scene of people and animal on the terraces, and the Tulou is surrounded by a soft mist and low hanging clouds.

◎ 把秧苗拔出来扎成一小撮。（赖永生 摄）
Uprooting the seedlings and bundling them up. (Photo by Lai Yongsheng)

耕耘收获的土楼金秋

　　春种夏长，秋收冬藏，土楼人在田野耕耘收获，生生不息。土楼的秋收时节是那么动人，土楼人家秋收的喜悦，就在那沉甸甸的稻谷上，就在那挂满红柿的树上，就在那绿油油的菜园中。

　　从土楼的高处向远处望去，那沿着山坡层层叠叠的梯田里，那满是金黄色的田野里，到处都是土楼人忙碌的身影。中壮年男女带着成群的孩子在田里挥汗如雨，大人们一边弯着腰挥动着镰刀，一边把手中的割下来的稻穗放到身旁；土楼里长大的孩子们自然也不甘示弱，他们稚嫩的小手也忙个不停，时而帮大人们把一捆捆的稻穗抱到打谷机旁，时而端着一碗凉凉的山泉水给大人们，时而还要照看着那些在稻田里面玩耍的比他们还年幼的弟弟妹妹。一拨一拨的土楼人穿梭在金灿灿的成堆的稻穗间和轰轰作响不停转动的打谷机旁，劳作着、谈笑着。乡间的小路上，或挑或抬，或提或扛，一担担、一袋袋的稻谷被农人们运回家。这样如火如荼的画面就像一幅巨大的油画美丽动人。

◎ 土楼四周的金色稻田。（苏永青 摄）
The golden fields around the Tulou. (Photo by Su Yongqing)

◎ 谷场欢歌。（赖永生 摄）
The golden fields overflow with laughter and chatter. (Photo by Lai Yongsheng)

The Golden Autumn

Sown in spring, tended to in summer. Harvested in autumn, stored in winter. Such is the cycle of agriculture. The Tulou people are busy harvesting all autumn long, a merry time when they reap the rewards of their efforts gone by. It is the simple things that bring joy: the now grown rice paddy, the bright red of the persimmons hanging on the trees, and the lush green of the vegetable garden.

Looking out from the Tulou, one can see the terraced paddocks, the golden fields and the hard working Tulou people. Parents and children alike sweat in the fields, the adults swinging their sickles and harvesting crops, before stacking them by the thresher. The teenagers and children put the crops near the thresher and run water to the adults. The golden fields overflow with laughter and chatter as the Tulou people labour away. The country roads become a river of people as they cart the grains back to the Tulou, and the whole countryside could be an oil painting.

每座土楼里，都能见到手动的稻谷风车。收割回来的稻谷倒进风车，土楼人呼啦啦地摇动，吹几遍，把干扁的谷壳吹走。妇人们打开约五米长三米宽竹子编成的席子，也称"谷笪"，把吹好的稻谷倒在上面，再用耙子铺开，开始晾晒。土楼顿时成了金色的世界。

这几年，土楼当地政府大力实施"乡村振兴"战略，积极探索乡村旅游引领乡村振兴的新路子，各地土楼群纷纷开展形式多样、丰富多彩的农民丰收节活动，让游客与当地农民一起体验丰收的喜悦，实地感受金色梯田上的农耕风情。

Each Tulou has its own winnower. The harvested grain is poured into this contraption, where the men get only plump grains by blowing away empty ones. The women place the golden grains onto a large mat, around 5 metres long and 3 metres wide, also known as a "Gu Yu", where the drying process begins. With these mats everywhere, the floors of the Tulou are like golden sand.

In recent years, the local government has been vigorously trying to "revitalise the countryside", particularly with regards to tourism in rural areas. Many local communities have launched farmers' harvest festivals, where tourists can experience the same pride and joy that farmers doing during harvesting season.

◎ 谷笪上晾晒稻谷。（赖永生 摄）
Drying grains on the mats. (Photo by Lai Yongsheng)

© 金秋柿子。（胡家新 摄）
Drying persimmons in autumn. (Photo by Hu Jiaxin)

◎ 老调不老。（王福平 摄）
Playing as skillfully as before. (Photo by Wang Fuping)

老当益壮的土楼老人

历尽沧桑的土楼里，老人们的脸上写满了岁月的痕迹。勤劳善良的一群老阿婆在土楼院子里，或忙着加工木薯、晾晒薯粉；或把一根根干净的地瓜、萝卜切成条，晾晒成地瓜干、萝卜干；或把一棵棵芥菜用盐巴揉搓，再拿到篱笆上挂起来晒干，或者搭配一些大蒜、辣椒塞到一个罐子里面密封起来，制作成别样的客家酸菜。阿婆们满是皱纹的手似乎有特别的魔力，加上传统的工艺，制作出来的客家酸菜和客家小菜，道道都是美味佳肴。

土楼里的老大爷自然也不示弱，身体硬朗的还能拿着镰刀扛着锄头干些农活；身体稍弱一些的，也会起早摸黑的赶着一头牛或者赶着一群鸭；身体再差一点的，也会干点杂活，编编篱笆，修修扫把，他们就这样天天在这座熟悉得不能再熟悉的村庄里绘出一幅幅忙碌的劳动画卷。

农忙时节，有时候为了赶时间收割稻子，土楼里的老大爷还会带着孩子往田间地头送茶送饭，老阿婆则会在楼门前的大坪上晾晒谷子。居住在土楼里面的老人们，只要身体还能活动，就一定要做点力所能及的事情，尽管他们儿孙满堂，衣食无忧，但他们就是闲不下那双勤劳的双手，这或许正是客家人祖祖辈辈留下的勤劳持家的传统吧。

◎ 老当益壮。（张耀辉 摄）

Old but strong. (Photo by Zhang Yaohui)

The Steadfast Elderly of the Tulou

The Tulou have a rich history, and it shows in the lines on the faces of its eldest residents. Kind, hard-working elderly women prepare food in the courtyard. They clean and prepare cassava, cut sweet potato and turnip, and dry them to store for later. They make Hakka sauerkraut from harvesting the vegetables to preserving them with spices. Their gentle, wrinkled hands seem to have a magic about them, as all the food they touch with years of experience turns out to be utterly delicious.

The elderly men are not ones to lose out to their partners either. Those who are still physically capable wield sickles and help out on the farm where they can. Others still wake up early in the morning to take care of the animals. Even those who are unable to do that help out where they can – mending fences, repairing tools and offering their support in this community that could not be tighter.

When the farm gets busy, in order to harvest in a timely manner, the elderly will sometimes take the kids to deliver food to the working adults, while others process the harvested grains. It seems that all of the elderly are determined to continue working and contribute whatever they can, a trait that has been passed down in this style of living for centuries.

守望家园的土楼儿女

　　一位从小就生活在土楼里的"70后"女子，从另外一个土楼村嫁到这个土楼村。她的家人都在土楼里经营土特产和茶叶。早年，她也跟许许多多农村青年一样离开家乡，外出打工，后来她放弃大城市的生活和工作，回到了土楼，当了一名土楼讲解员。用她的话说，她喜欢祖祖辈辈居住过的土楼，她习惯了土楼里悠闲的生活，对土楼有着非常深厚的感情。在给游客讲解时，她一边正儿八经地为游客讲解土楼，一边风趣地为游客讲述土楼故事，讲述她在土楼成长过程中的所见所闻，时不时还为游客们献上一两首客家山歌，经常让游客们笑得人仰马翻，大家都很喜欢这个长得漂亮能说会唱的"土导游"（土生土长的土楼讲解员的趣称）。

　　看得出来，每当她为游客推介家乡的土楼、宣传土楼文化时，脸上都洋溢出幸福和自豪的笑容。她时常说的一句话就是："能够把家乡的土楼通过自己告诉给世界各地的游客，这是我引以为荣的一件事。"在土楼里面，经常可以看到像这位"70后"女子一样的"土导游"，她们当中一些是土楼长大的"土楼女儿"，一些是嫁到土楼里的"土楼媳妇"。她们靓丽的身影、娓娓道来的讲述，跟美丽的土楼融为一体，向世界展现神奇美丽的土楼！

◎　"土导游"阿才和外国游客。（阿才 供图）
　Local tour guide A'cai and a foreign tourist. (Courtesy of A'cai)

The Returning Children of the Tulou

There is a young woman, born in the 1970s, who is married into this Tulou from another Tulou. Her family works selling local goods and tea. In earlier years, she and many other adolescents left the Tulou to find work in urban areas. However, she left her job in the city and returned to the Tulou, where she is now a tour guide. In her own words, she loves that generations live together in the Tulou, she much prefers the relaxed lifestyle, and she feels a deep connection to the Tulou. When giving tours, she delivers informative speeches regarding the Tulou, but at the same time, weaves in her own childhood experiences. Occasionally, she will even burst into folk songs, delighting the tour group. Needless to say, she receives glowing reviews.

Her pride for her home is clear to see on her face as she welcomes tourists. She often says, "it is my privilege to be able to be a conduit by which the Tulou is shared with the world." There are many other young women like her that act as tour guides, including both those who grew up in the Tulou as well as those who married in later. Their enthusiasm, storytelling and passion blend are a fantastic lens through which the outside world sees the Tulou.

◎ 满怀憧憬的年轻一代。（赖永生 摄）
Hopeful young generation. (Photo by Lai Yongsheng)

◎ 土楼名人阿耕。（赖永生 摄）
A'geng, a Tulou celebrity. (Photo by Lai Yongsheng)

2008年"福建土楼"申遗成功后，很多像这位"70后"土楼姑娘一样的年轻男女，纷纷放弃城里的工作生活，返乡创业。有的成为当地的导游，有的办起了土楼旅馆、开起了土楼饭店，有的传承了当地的手艺，制作土楼米酒、柿子饼等土特产和工艺品，有的则专门从事土楼文艺表演或土楼文化研究，有的还在淘宝网上开起了网店推广家乡的土特产和手工艺品。他们不管从事生意经营还是宣传土楼文化，一个共同点就是"原生态"。他们将现代生活元素跟古老的土楼融合在一起，让已历经数十年、数百年的土楼显得更有生机、更有活力！

受益于土楼保护的还有许多坚守土楼的楼主们，其中不得不说到一位"土楼名人"——永定洪坑土楼群振成楼楼主之一林日耕，人称"阿耕"。小学毕业的他从最初地地道道的农民到小商贩，再到土楼"义务讲解员"，他做起了土楼旅游的生意，全家人都吃起了"土楼饭"。他的家人在土楼里做餐饮住宿生意，卖土楼纪念品，自己则是福建客家土楼旅游有限公司的特邀导游员。经常用本地话加普通话向国内外游客介绍土楼建筑、土楼历史和土楼人文，宣传土楼文化。在土楼里，他给党和国家领导人以及联合国官员和外国著名专家做过讲解员。

如今，祖祖辈辈留传的土楼成了世界文化遗产，一方面改善了土楼人的生活，让坚守土楼、回归家乡的土楼儿女们摆脱贫困走向小康生活；另外一方面也让他们更加有能力和信心守护好土楼、传承好土楼文化！

© 土楼媳妇的坚守。（冯木波 摄）
Tulou women's business. (Photo by Feng Mubo)

In 2008, after Fujian Tulou was added to the UNESCO's World Heritage List, many adolescents who had left Tulou for urban areas abandoned their life in the city and returned home. Some became tour guides, some opened hotels and restaurants and some became apprentices to traditional practices like the making of rice wine, persimmon cakes and other local crafts. Some even began using platforms like Taobao to market local products. Regardless of whether they started businesses or if they promote culture, they are part of bringing attention to the Tulou in an authentic way. Those that returned have brought with them modern ways of living, and this, incorporated into the traditional Tulou lifestyle, which has brought even more energy into an already vibrant community.

The efforts to maintain Tulou culture are also largely in part to famous Tulou community members. One such member can be considered a Tulou celebrity–Lin Rigeng, from Zhenchenglou. After primary school, he worked as a farmer, then a small business owner, before getting involved with the Tulou community as a leader. From there, he expanded upon Tulou tourism, opening a bed and breakfast type accommodation, where he also sold Tulou souvenirs. He is a special tour guide for Fujian Hakka Tulou Tourism Company and can be seen taking tours in both Hakka and mandarin, explaining the rich culture of Tulou. He has even given tours to multiple party and state leaders, as well as United Nations officials and other foreign dignitaries.

Today, Fujian Tulou is a humble way of living for many generations, and has been recognised as world cultural heritage. This has improved the life of the Tulou people and allowed for the younger generation to make a better living at home despite a rapidly changing world. It has also allowed for the preservation of Tulou culture and heritage, which its residents can now proudly pass on to their next generation.

© 如诗如画的土楼家园。（冯木波 摄）
Picturesque home land. (Photo by Feng Mubo)

土楼风情——世代传承的民俗文化

土楼节庆与民俗活动

■ 土楼人家过大年

土楼人最重视春节，总是早早就开始准备了。春节前十多天，家家户户就都放下了手中的农活，把家里的每个角落彻底打扫干净，清洗桌凳等家具，俗称"扫屋"。

从农历十二月二十五开始，俗称"入年假"，要祭祀灶神。家家户户开始备好糖果、水果等年货，有的开始杀年猪馈赠亲朋好友；有的开始蒸年糕，做芋子包、菜丝粄等等。

除夕当天，大家忙着准备过年的鸡鸭鱼肉。上午祭拜神明，张贴对联年画，张灯结彩；再上宗祠祭拜祖先。下午两三点钟后，便满院子都在热热闹闹地张罗年夜饭了。

◎ 环极楼里贴春联。（胡家新 摄）

Putting up New Year couplets in Huanjilou. (Photo by Hu Jiaxin)

Tulou Folk Culture

Tulou Festivals and Folk Activities

■ Celebrating the Spring Festival

For Tulou people, the most important festival of the year is the Spring Festival which celebrates the beginning of the lunar New Year. Festivities always begin early, sometimes starting from more than ten days out from the date. Every household has completed their farm work, thoroughly cleaned every corner and wiped down all the tables and chairs as is common practice in the lead up to the lunar New Year.

The holiday period begins from the lunar calendar's 25th day of the twelfth month. It is necessary to pay respects to the kitchen god and start preparing the New Year candy and fruits. Gift giving and preparation for popular dishes such as steamed rice cakes and dumplings also happen around this time.

On New Year's Eve, the day begins with prayers to the gods, worshipping their ancestors, putting up New Year couplets and pictures, and decorating with lanterns and colored hangings. In the afternoon, families get the courtyard ready for the lunar New Year dinner which no doubt will feature the chicken, duck and fish dishes prepared earlier on.

◎ 振成楼舞龙。（胡家新 摄）

Dragon dance at Zhenchenglou. (Photo by Hu Jiaxin)

◎ 盛大的年夜饭。（冯木波 摄）
The grand dinner at New Year's Eve. (Photo by Feng Mubo)

　　年夜饭是一年中最隆重、最丰盛的团圆饭，美味佳肴不计其数，但土楼人的年夜饭上，必不可少鸡、豆腐和鱼三样菜，"鸡"与"吉"谐音，寓意"吉祥如意"，鸡头象征"头彩"；"腐"寓意"富"，"鱼"与"余"谐音，寓意"富贵有余"。

　　土楼人的年夜饭还有一些有趣的讲究，其中最重要的是最年长者一定要坐上位，然后按辈分往下排；晚辈要逐一给长辈夹菜、敬酒、道祝福；饭桌上不能把鱼全吃光，要留些第二天吃，寓意"年年有余（鱼）"。团圆饭吃完，已经工作的晚辈给长辈包个红包，表示孝敬；长辈给还没收入的孩子压岁钱，祝福孩子健康长大，学业有成。

The lunar New Year's Eve dinner is always grand with families reuniting together on this special occasion. There are countless dishes that will make mouths water from the sight and the smell. It is essential that chicken, tofu, and fish are present on the dinner table. The Chinese characters for each of these items are homophonic to characters that mean good luck and fortune.

There are some special rules and traditions that must be observed in Tulou. The most important is that the eldest member of the family will always be at the head of the table. The chairs will then be filled up according to seniority. The younger generation should always help the elders to food and wine, and drink a toast to them with best wishes. The fish must not be finished; it is necessary to leave some for the next day. This symbolizes a saying in Chinese that means there to be more in the new year. After the reunion dinner is over, those of the younger generation who are in employment, will have prepared red envelops for their elders to express filial piety while the elders give the youngest children, who have not yet reached working age, red envelops with lucky money inside. These come with the hopes and wishes that the children will grow up healthily and have successful futures.

除夕晚上，土楼人要"守岁"到天明。除夕夜11点以后，土楼人家都要挑好时辰"开大门"，大家纷纷打开土楼的大门和厨房门，朝着吉利方向用香火祭拜神明，祭拜之后，燃放长长的鞭炮，表示辞旧迎新、迎春接福。

大年初一，男女老少穿上新衣服，互相拜年，逢人说好话；大年初二走亲访友；大年初三全家动手大扫除，扫得越干净越好，俗称"扫穷鬼"；大年初四开始"闹新年"或者走亲访友；大年初五"开小正"（客家话）以后便可以开始外出干活了，在外地工作的年轻人，也将陆陆续续离开土楼，去土楼外的世界打拼。

On the Eve, the Tulou locals will stay up until dawn. After eleven o'clock at night, they must pick a good time to open every door within their building and then worship the gods with incense while facing an auspicious direction. After their prayers, long firecrackers are lit up as a way to symbolize the old welcoming the new with a bang.

On the first day of the lunar New Year, everyone will put on new clothes and greet each other with well wishes. Then on the second day, families will visit their extended relatives and friends. On the third day, the family will tidy up, the cleaner the better as it is meant to bring good fortune. The fourth day is for visiting relatives and friends again while on the fifth day, people will go back out to work.

◎ 给长辈拜年。（赖永生 摄）
Saying Happy New Year to the elders. (Photo by Lai Yongsheng)

　　整个节日，每座土楼都绽放着节日的欢乐：敲锣打鼓、舞龙舞狮、载歌载舞、燃放鞭炮、吃饭喝酒，热闹非凡。

　　春节期间，龙岩市永定土楼景区会举办"我在永定土楼过大年"等主题活动，邀请游客到土楼里一起感受土楼过年的氛围，让游客现场体验生土夯墙的营造技艺，举办民间绝艺表演、土楼艺术团表演、木偶戏表演、客家婚嫁表演等。漳州市南靖土楼景区，除了举办一些体验过大年的各种主题活动以外，有的地方还会举办一些独具当地特色的民俗活动，如土楼腰鼓、大鼓凉伞、舞龙舞狮等精彩表演，为土楼的春节增添了浓厚的年味。

◎ 田螺坑的除夕夜。（冯木波 摄）
The New Year's Eve at Tianluokeng Tulou Cluster.
(Photo by Feng Mubo)

Every Tulou is full of festive joy during the Spring Festival celebrations. There is the beating of drums, dancing dragons and lions, people singing and dancing, eating and drinking as well as the firecrackers being set off. It is truly a lively and extraordinary atmosphere.

During the Spring Festival holiday period, the scenic spots within Yongding Tulou area will hold an event that invites tourists to visit the Tulou and experience the local New Year festivities first hand. There are many performances to show the culture such as folk dance and music, puppet shows and other forms of art. By holding a variety of themed activities to give visitors the full Spring Festival experience, the atmosphere becomes even more vibrant as everyone can celebrate together.

　　每年的农历正月十一，在永定坎市镇，卢氏后裔都会举办独特的客家传统民俗活动"打新婚"，这种习俗已有500多年的历史。这一天，从周边乡镇赶来做客的、看热闹的人络绎不绝。中午时分，大家酒足饭饱以后，便会纷纷赶到卢氏大宗祠。现场拼起几张八仙桌作为祭坛，上面摆着各种各样的供品。唢呐、管弦声、铳炮声响起，一排排上一年结婚的新婚夫妻面对祖宗牌位焚香祭拜，一位由大家推举的德高望重的长辈代表（俗称"酒醉公"），在两个壮汉的搀扶下，手上拿着一根纸做的写着"早生贵子"的红滚筒（俗称"面槌"），对着新郎官的肩膀、背部上下"捶打"（滚动），口中念着"早生贵子"等祝福语。一个个新婚男子被众人推着给"酒醉公""捶打"。此时，震耳欲聋的鞭炮声和此起彼伏的欢笑声把"打新婚"活动推向高潮。

◎ 打新婚活动现场热闹非凡。（王福平 摄）
The unique celebration. (Photo by Wang Fuping)

◎ 打新婚。（王福平 摄）
Blissfully beating the newlyweds. (Photo by Wang Fuping)

■ Beating the Newlyweds at Kanshi

In the first lunar month, the descendants of the Lu family clan will hold a unique Hakka traditional folklore event in Kanshi, Yongding. The idea behind the celebration can be interpreted literally into "blissfully beating the newlyweds". In essence, it is a chance to bless them to have a baby soon, a tradition which has a history of more than 500 years. On this day, people from surrounding towns and villages come to attend. At noon, once everyone has eaten to their belly's content, they will rush to the Lu ancestral hall. There, tables covered in various offerings have been pre-assembled. Many sounds can be heard such as the clash of cymbals and orchestral sounds as the couples who have recently married within the last year line up in a row and face the worship stand. A highly respected elder representative, with the help of two strong men, will hold up a red scroll with the words "Have a baby soon" written on, and "beat" the new husbands on the back and shoulder as he blesses the couple with children. Once this has been completed, the deafening sounds of firecrackers and laughter fill the air.

◎ 张灯结彩迎花灯。（冯木波 摄）
Parade of dragons and lanterns. (Photo by Feng Mubo)

■ 张灯结彩闹元宵

正月十五是元宵节。元宵节当天，家家户户祭拜神明、燃放鞭炮、吃汤圆。有的地方会举办闹花灯、舞龙舞狮、敲锣打鼓、走古事和猜灯谜等形式多样、丰富多彩的闹元宵活动。有些地方还有上灯、贴名单的习俗。

土楼各地闹元宵的民俗活动也异彩纷呈。当人们在元宵节的晚上来到土楼，可以在当地村落的各个祠堂里看到土楼人家在焚香拜祖、张灯结彩。永定土楼闹元宵迎花灯活动别具特色，有的地方从正月十三或十四开始，闹元宵至正月十六或十七日结束。夜幕降临，各路花灯在火牌、锣鼓的引导下出发，井然有序地在本地村落巡游，有的到附近村落的同宗族聚居地巡游。每到一个祠堂，大家都要祭祀祖宗。大约三四个小时以后，花灯队伍敲锣打鼓分别回到各自祖楼厅堂，并向各家各户"送灯"，寓意添丁兴旺。"接灯"的人家要在门口燃放鞭炮，把灯悬挂在家里直到第二天天亮，并将准备好的酒菜、糖果拿出来招待送灯人和其他客人。元宵节整个晚上灯火通明、热闹非凡。

■ Celebrating the Lantern Festival

According to the lunar calendar, the fifteenth day of the first lunar month is the Lantern Festival. Because it also marks the last day of the Spring Festival, there is great importance placed on the day. Families will pay their respects to the gods, set off firecrackers and eat delicious glutinous rice balls. In some places, there are various kinds of celebratory activities such as lantern exhibitions, dragon and lion dancing, beating drums and riddle guessing. Customs will vary from village to village with some hanging up lights, or writing their wishes on the lanterns before setting them afloat.

The Tulou people have always regarded the Lantern Festival with great importance. When people arrive at the Tulou in the evening, they will notice all the burning incense as families pay their respects to the ancestors. The festival at the Yongding Tulou has its own specialties. Some areas will start celebrating on the 13th or 14th day until the 16th or 17th day. As night falls, the beating of the drums starts as a team of lantern bearers lead a parade among the local villages. The parade which also includes dragon and lion dancers make the long line seem as if it is one whole dragon weaving through the streets and between the Tulou, a very spectacular sight. Every time they passed an ancestral hall, everyone has to pay their respects. About three or four hours later, the lantern bearers will go to their respective ancestral halls to "deliver light", an action symbolic of bringing in prosperity to their households. Each Tulou the lanterns arrive at, must "receive the light" by setting off firecrackers and treating the guests with tea and candies. It is customary to hang the lanterns at home until the next morning.

◎ 环极楼里舞龙。（陈军 摄）
Dragon dance in Huanjilou. (Photo by Chen Jun)

◎ 田螺坑里的舞龙。（冯木波 摄）
Dragon dance in Tianluokeng Tulou Cluster. (Photo by Feng Mubo)

　　南靖土楼闹元宵的习俗也是以闹花灯、舞龙舞狮为主。元宵节当晚，上一年度结婚生子的新婚夫妇要带着供品和一个点上灯火的红灯，抱着新生男孩到祖祠焚香拜祖，答谢祖先保佑。祭拜以后，还要把红灯带回家里悬挂，寓意新的一年"丁财两旺"。除了这个古老而又神圣的习俗以外，当地还有舞龙舞狮、表演芗剧或木偶戏的活动，异常热闹。

　　有些土楼人家举行龙艺表演，龙艺表演的龙头、龙尾的扎制、装饰跟传统的"舞龙"差不多，龙身由竹、木、纸、绢等材料扎成楼、阁、舟、车模样的几十块木艺板组成，每块木艺板上站着一位装扮成戏曲人物的童男童女，由两位壮汉用肩膀扛着。这些衣着形状各异的童男童女，与龙身上的花卉草虫鱼、彩灯融为一体，十分壮观。浩浩荡荡的龙艺表演所到之处，人们都要点起香烛、燃放鞭炮，一边欢迎龙艺表演带来的吉祥，一边尽情享受不一样的节日气氛。

The people of Nanjing Tulou also celebrate predominantly with decorative lanterns as well as dancing dragons and lions. On the night of the festival, newlyweds from the previous year who have had children must bring their newborn boys, offerings and a red lantern to their ancestors. Here, they will burn incense and pray to their ancestors to give thanks for their blessings. After paying their respects, the red lantern will be taken back and hung up for good fortune. Apart from this tradition, there are many activities ranging from dragon and lion dancing, live drama performances and puppet shows, all adding to the lively environment.

Some Tulou locals also showcase large installations featuring dragon lanterns, mini pavilions, buildings and cars. The dragons have decorated heads and tails, made of bamboo, paper and other materials while the rest of the display is made from crafted wooden boards. Strong men carry children dressed as opera characters on their shoulders, their costumes decorated with flowers and nature scenes, forming a splendid sight to see. Wherever there are these wonderful displays, there will be people lighting incense sticks and setting off firecrackers to welcome auspiciousness into the year while at the same time, enjoying the joyous celebrations.

◎ 龙艺表演。（冯木波 摄）
A dragon show with children on shoulders. (Photo by Feng Mubo)

■ 永定抚市走古事

在永定抚市镇，"抚市迎花灯走古事"闹元宵的民俗活动从农历正月十三到正月十七，连续五天时间。抚市迎花灯时，人们一边举着形形色色的花灯，一边跳着优美的舞步，队形变化多端，这就是抚市迎花灯的特色。当地村民把人们喜闻乐见的历代传说故事、戏曲《桃园三结义》《七仙女下凡》《八仙过海》等十几个古事棚由一队一队的青壮年抬着走起来，到处巡游，阵容庞大、节目众多、服饰华丽、演技出众，场面非常壮观。

■ Fushi, Yongding – Bringing Ancient Folk Tales Alive

In Fushi, Yongding, the town will put up lanterns displays while passing on the traditions of ancient folk tales. The celebration lasts from the 13th day of the first lunar month until the 17th day. People hold up many different shaped lanterns while dancing in a varied formation – a uniquely Fushi style of celebrating. The local villagers will bring famous and popular folk tales to life through re-enactments. The staging and costumes are spectacular with people coming and going to admire the illuminating shows.

◎ 壮观的走古事队伍。（胡家新 摄）
Ancient story show in Fushi. (Photo by Hu Jiaxin)

◎ 可爱的小演员。（胡家新 摄）

Lovely players. (Photo by Hu Jiaxin)

◎ 龙出承启楼。（胡家新 摄）

Dragon dance in Chengqilou. (Photo by Hu Jiaxin)

■ 永定高头乡舞龙灯

在永定高头乡，"舞龙灯"闹元宵的节目也是精彩绝伦。高头乡五个村数以千计的村民，大多同祖共宗，舞龙灯是他们闹祖祠的传统，寓意闹丁闹财，丁财两旺。各村都会竭尽所能，做出一两条代表本村水平的龙，到祖祠前献技献艺。舞龙灯的时间从正月十四持续到正月十六。正月十五元宵节之夜，全乡的龙灯从七点半开始集中到高头乡高东祖祠表演，然后依次到高北、高南祖祠表演，长龙戏珠，龙鼓伴奏，舞动热烈奔放，技巧变化多端，或腾云驾雾，或波涛翻滚。各村舞者无不拿出绝活，希望自己技高一筹，力压群龙。各村的龙灯队伍除了拜祭祖宗神明，还到一座一座土楼舞龙。楼主们燃放长长的鞭炮，欢天喜地迎接一条又一条龙灯，让土楼增添了节日的喜庆，也让土楼有了龙的势头，来年兴旺有望。

■ Gaotou, Yongding – Dancing Dragons

In Gaotou, Yongding, dragon dancing plays an important role in their festivities. Thousands of villagers from five villages in the area have mutual ancestors who have always kept this tradition. Every village will have at least one or two dragons representing them to perform for the ancestors between the 14th and the 16th day of the first lunar month. On the night of the 15th, all the dancing dragons will congregate from seven thirty in the evening in Gaotou to perform. What a sight it is to behold, the variety of dragons weaving through the crowds, the drumming accompaniment as people dance freely, and the imitation of floating clouds or rolling waves! All the village dancers will come up with unique ways to present their dragon lanterns, creating a scenery of duelling dancing dragons. In addition to worshiping the gods, the dragons will visit each Tulou and perform the dragon dance. The hosts from each Tulou will greet the dragons by setting off long firecrackers, building up the joyous atmosphere and in hopes that it will bring the Tulou great fortune.

◎ 力压群龙。（张耀辉 摄）
Amazing dragon dance. (Photo by Zhang Yaohui)

■ 永定下洋迎花灯

　　"下洋中川迎花灯"是著名侨乡永定下洋重大的民俗活动。"迎灯"与迎丁谐音，寓意人丁兴旺。中川迎花灯可分为炒灯、写灯、制灯、迎灯、接灯、吃灯酒等几个环节。迎灯是闹元宵民俗活动的重头戏。夜幕降临，各路花灯在火牌、锣鼓的引导下，游遍已经定好的线路。一路上，各种各样的花灯在夜色中井然有序地游走，像一条长长的火龙，穿行在中川村的几座土楼间，异常壮观。穿过三五回合以后，所有花灯在中川村的后山、广场上摆开展览。

　　一阵喧闹以后，便开始"烧花"，这是"闹灯"的高潮，只见条条火龙腾空而起，一声声脆响之后，土楼的夜空绽放出万般银花。"烧花"之后，花灯队伍敲锣打鼓分别回到各自祖楼厅堂，这是"回灯"；之后分头派人去各家"送灯"，所到人家要燃放鞭炮来"接灯"，并向送灯人端茶递烟，互致吉祥。有的人家备上好酒好菜款待送灯人，谓之"吃灯酒"，一番热闹祝福之后，一年一度的元宵节闹花灯活动才算落下帷幕。

◎ 长长的火龙。（胡剑文 摄）
A long dragon of lanterns. (Photo by Hu Jianwen)

◎ 中川花灯。（冯木波 摄）
The Lantern Festival in Zhongchuan. (Photo by Feng Mubo)

■ Xiayang, Yongding – Welcoming the Lanterns

The Lantern Festival is one of the most important celebrations in the year in Zhongchuan, Xiayang. It is a time for the locals to give their hopes and wishes for a prosperous year ahead. The activities that occur include writing on lanterns, making lanterns, the process of welcoming lanterns and the consumption of festival food. By welcoming the lights, it highlights one of the most popular folk activities that happen during the Lantern Festival. When night falls, a line of lantern installations light up around a pathway as the sound of gongs and drums rise. Along the way, you can pass all kinds of lantern displays, such as the shape of a long dragon weaving its way through Zhongchuan Village. Once all the lights have been paraded through the village a couple of times, they will be showcased in the back hills and squares of Zhongchuan Village.

After this period of festivities, it is time to burn the lanterns – the climax of celebration as the sky is illuminated with sparks. After completing this ritual, the lantern performers beat the drums as everyone returns back to their respective ancestral halls. This is known as "returning the light". After that, people "send the light" to each household where it will be greeted with firecrackers and people handing out cigarettes and offering tea. Some families will prepare good wine and food to be given to the lantern bearers. Once blessings have been given and respects paid to the ancestors, the Lantern Festival comes to an end.

■ 华安大地土楼三月三

三月三是华安大地土楼群沿袭了200多年的民俗活动。每年农历三月三，居住在华安大地土楼群的蒋氏宗亲都要将祖祖辈辈敬奉的主神——玄天上帝请出玄天阁，巡社游香，穿行全村，以此祈求来年风调雨顺，五谷丰登。巡游的队伍中，还有民俗表演队、大旗队、大鼓凉伞队、锣鼓队、鞭炮队、响铳队等等，组成一条土楼民俗文化长龙。游香队伍所到之处，可以看见当地村民摆上供品、点燃香烛、燃放鞭炮。家家户户除了备好鸡鸭鱼肉和各类糖果等供品，还会特地制作当地的特色美食鼠曲粿。整个大地村气球高悬，鞭炮轰鸣，锣鼓喧天，人头攒动，异常热闹。下午巡游结束以后，村民便会把玄天上帝护送回到玄天阁。玄天阁四周，华安土楼群的广场或者天井里，都会上演精彩纷呈的民俗表演。每年的土楼三月三，华安大地土楼群旅居海外的蒋姓族人也会回到土楼，跟族人团聚的同时，共同庆贺这个古老而又神圣的节日。

◎ 大地土楼三月三。（胡家新 摄）
The god parade on the third day of the third lunar month. (Photo by Hu Jiaxin)

■ Dadi Tulou – The Third Day of the Third Lunar Month

This has been a custom in Hua'an Dadi Tulou Cluster for over 200 years. Every year, on the third day of the third month during the lunar year, the Jiang clan who reside at Hua'an Tulou must pay their respects to the gods as they have for many generations. The people pray and light incense as they carry the god idol from Xuantian Pavilion to parade around the village so that it may bless them with good weather and grain harvest in the year ahead. As part of the parade, there are folk performances, flag bearing teams, large drums and firecrackers. This is so that the god is accompanied throughout the process. Wherever this parade went, local villagers can be seen putting out offerings, lighting incense sticks and setting off firecrackers. In addition, every household prepares chicken, duck, fish, all kinds of sweets and special cakes with their own local twist. The village is a lively place to be with the drumming, crackling firecrackers and moving crowds. In the afternoon, the villagers will escort the god back to Xuantian Pavilion. Around the pavilion, there is a large square where performances will continue. During this time of the year, many members of the Jiang clan living abroad will return to Hua'an Tulou to celebrate the festival together, a reunion of the past and present.

■ 永定陈东四月八

"陈东四月八"是永定陈东乡几百年来传统的民俗活动，从农历四月初七到初九，以初八那天最为隆重，十几个方阵组成的队伍在锣鼓喧天、铳炮连连的公路上缓缓移动，场面浩浩荡荡。"陈东四月八"祭拜的是"玉封公王"谢安（东晋名相），谢安曾帮助过永定陈东乡的卢氏祖先，所以当地人为了报答恩人，便奉谢安为神。活动开始之日，"玉封公王"由陈东广圣庙出巡，沿途十几个村分别设一个供坛，所到之处，村民顶礼膜拜，祈求风调雨顺、合家平安。

"陈东四月八"既是乡民表达感恩的庆典，又是民间文艺的大展示。乐队、锣鼓队乐鼓喧天，舞龙、舞狮队妙趣横生，彩车、演员热闹非凡，《小丑逗乐》《猪八戒背新娘》《孙悟空耍棍棒》等传统故事被演绎得惟妙惟肖。

◎ 振成楼舞龙。（胡家新 摄）
Dragon dance at Zhenchenglou. (Photo by Hu Jiaxin)

◎ "玉封公王"出巡。（胡家新 摄）
The parade of the statue of Xie An. (Photo by Hu Jiaxin)

■ Chendong, Yongding – The Eighth Day of the Fourth Lunar Month

A century year old custom of Chendong Town in Yongding is to celebrate on the eighth day of the fourth lunar month. This starts from the seventh day until the ninth day, with the most importance being placed on the eighth. A parade of gongs and drums follows up a road, drawing a large amount of attention to their mighty presence. The festival is for worshiping Xie An (a famous prime minister around 1,600 years ago), who was believed to have helped the Lu clan's ancestors. On the day, the parade will start from Chendong Guangsheng Temple. Many villages will set up altars and wherever the parade goes, the villagers will pray for good weather and family harmony.

This day is not only for the villagers to show their gratitude, but a day to showcase folk art. The band, the gongs, the drums, and the dragon and lion dance teams create a large display. Traditional folk stories are vividly interpreted and put on show.

◎ 备好粽叶。（冯木波 摄）
Preparing bamboo leaves to make *zongzi*.
(Photo by Feng Mubo)

■ 春夏之交端午节

农历五月初五端午节，土楼客家人亦称为端阳节、五月节，是春夏之交最重要的节日。

从四月底开始，人们就开始筹划过端午节。要上山采粽叶，采葛藤、菖蒲、艾叶等备用。五月初三开始，忙于包煮粽子、杀猪宰羊、打鱼捉虾、杀鸡鸭鹅兔等等。五月初四之前，男人尤其是男童要剃头，初四下午全家人都要以艾叶、菖蒲等煎汤沐浴，浴毕以雄黄酒点涂头顶、太阳穴、心窝、肚脐等部位，每人都要喝鱼腥草等草药汤，喝雄黄酒，据说可防端午前后最为活跃的蛇。

初五当天，儿童要穿新衣，佩戴香囊、菖蒲及艾叶，大人拜完神，就可吃粽子。午饭就是过节，很丰盛。饭后到河边看赛龙舟或参与游泳比赛。无论男女，均首次被允许下河游泳。有的人带去粽子投入河中祭奠河神或屈原。

下午，妇女们还要结伴上山采集中草药茶。主要采集两类，一类是"粗茶"，包括高山茶叶、枇杷叶、枫叶、暑仙甘叶等等，晒干后煮大碗茶用；一类是"凉茶"，包括茅根、麦冬、野菊花、金银花、金钱草、鱼腥草、篱下青、满天星、黄鸡脚等，既可防病又可治病。两类草药茶土楼客家人称之为"午时茶"，民谚有云："午时茶，好做药。"人们相信端午节采集的午时茶可以除百病。

初六、初七，土楼客家人要走亲戚。这是春节元宵之后亲戚朋友间首次正式拜访，因而也少不了开怀畅饮，隆重热闹。

■ Dragon Boat Festival – The Turn of Spring and Summer

The fifth day of the fifth lunar month, is known as the Dragon Boat Festival. It marks the change between spring to summer.

From the end of the fourth month, people begin to plan the Dragon Boat Festival. It is necessary to go up the mountain to pick wild leaves and various herbs. On the third day of the fifth month, people are busy preparing foods such as *zongzi*, a pyramid-shaped glutinous rice dumpling wrapped in bamboo leaves, meats and seafood. Before the fourth day, males, particularly young boys, will shave their heads. In the afternoon of the fourth day, the whole family bathe in water mixed with herbs such as wormwood and calamus. After bathing, realgar wine is smeared on certain body parts such as the head, the temple, the heart and the navel. Everyone should drink herbal soup or realgar wine, which is said to prevent snakes who are most active around the time of the Dragon Boat Festival.

On the fifth day, children wear new clothes with fragrance pouches filled with calamus and wormwood. Once the adults have paid their respects to the gods, they come together and eat *zongzi*. Unlike the Spring Festival, lunch is the celebration meal and it is very extravagant. After lunch, dragon boat racing and swimming competitions begin at the river. Any one is allowed to go into the water and swim. Some people throw *zongzi* into the water for the river god and Qu Yuan.

In the afternoon, women will go into the mountains to collect Chinese herbs for tea. There are two types of tea to be gathered, the first is more course which includes items such as tea leaves found in the alpine areas, loquat leaves and maple leaves, which are dried in the sun before being brewed into a large pot of tea. The other type is for cool herbal tea such as wild chrysanthemum, honey suckle and ophiopogon japonicas. These are meant to have preventative and healing properties against diseases. Both types of tea have medicinal properties and folklore has it that the tea can prevent all diseases if collected during the Dragon Boat Festival.

On the sixth and seventh days, the Hakka people go to visit their relatives. This is known to be the first official visit between friends and relatives after the Spring Festival and Lantern Festival, so it is an important affair full of food and drinks.

■ 立秋前后中元节

农历七月十五是中国民间传统中元节，土楼客家人一般称之为七月半或七月节。

七月半是土楼客家人夏季收割之后的第一个节日，时间一般在立秋前后，夏种也基本结束。虽然新酒还没来得及酿造，但新禾米已登场，饥荒已解除，所以人们有过节的愿望。加上这个时候，鸡鸭成群，鱼肥虾多，蔬菜水果也盛产丰收，食材丰富，人们于是可以把这个节日过得较丰盛。

七月半又是土楼客家人祭祖的节日。土楼人家一般有春秋二祭。春祭在元宵前后，祭后男人可以外出谋生；秋祭则在七月半开始，至中秋前后。秋祭习俗其实也符合中国传统的秋尝祭祖习俗，夏季丰收了，用新禾米粄和自产的鸡鸭鱼祭祖，告慰先人，祈求保佑丰衣足食。

有少量姓氏在七月十四日过节，据说是因为宋代末年，人们正准备过节时，元兵突然来犯。为躲避元兵，人们匆匆将备好的食材于十四日先祭祖后即过节。此后该习俗沿袭下来。也有的地方说是因为躲避土匪抢劫而提前过节。

节后几天，亲戚朋友互相走访。有的人家用新禾米酿出的黄酒也起缸了，大家也可以尝新、痛饮。

◎ 做米酒。（刘宝生 摄）

Making rice wine. (Photo by Liu Baosheng)

◎ 盛大的祭祀。（王福平 摄 ）
Grand worshiping. (Photo by Wang Fuping)

■ The Ghost Festival

The fifteenth day of the seventh lunar month is known as the Ghost Festival. It is the first festival after the summer harvest and marks the changeover from summer to autumn.

Although the new wine has not yet aged enough, after working hard during the harvest, people are now ready for the holidays. In addition, poultry, seafood, vegetables and fruits are in abundance, making the celebrations more lavish.

The Ghost Festival is also a time for the families in the Tulou to pay their respects to their ancestors. The Tulou people usually have two important time of sacrifice, one in spring around the Lantern Festival, after which the men go out to work. The other in autumn begins around the time of the Ghost Festival and go until the Mid-Autumn Festival. These customs are also in line with the traditional Chinese traditions of honouring the ancestors during the autumn. After the summer harvest, granary, chicken, duck and fish are all brought in front of the ancestors to thank them for the blessings.

Very few people celebrate on the fourteenth day however, and folk tales say this is because in the early years of the Song Dynasty, people were preparing for the festival when suddenly, Yuan soldiers came and attacked. In order to avoid the soldiers, the people first visited their ancestors before having their celebrations. This custom has since passed through generations. Some would even say this is to avoid robberies prior to the festival.

A few days after the festival, relatives and friends will visit each other. Some people will bring freshly fermented rice wine for everyone to taste.

◎ 平和土楼放心愿灯。（冯木波 摄 ）

Lighting up the lantern with wishes in Pinghe. (Photo by Feng Mubo)

■ 团团圆圆过中秋

农历八月十五是中国乃至包括东亚、东南亚等地的中华传统文化圈的中秋节，土楼客家人则称之为八月节或八月半。

八月半是夏收夏种大忙之后土楼客家人最重要的节日。这时，进入农闲时节，土楼客家人也大多完成秋祭，男人们又将外出打工挣钱，家人要团聚一下。土楼人除了准备月饼和拜月的水果、柚子外，还要做甜粄、酿米酒，吃个丰盛的月半晚餐，即所谓"年朝午节月半夜"——大年初一早餐过节，端午节午餐过节，七月半八月半晚餐过节。

中秋节晚餐酒足饭饱之后，土楼客家人还有很重要的内容——团团圆圆守月华，即全家大人小孩都要聚集在土楼外天井或大门外，摆上八仙桌，每张八仙桌上都摆上月饼、柚子、糖果等，不用荤酒，正对月亮出来的那边摆上装满大米的米升做的香炉。家家围坐一桌，对月焚香祭拜后，就可以品尝月饼、柚子等，观赏月景。土楼人家在圆圆的月亮下面，在围合的土楼里面，吃着圆圆的月饼，这真是一个月圆楼圆人团圆的土楼中秋的独特场面。

有些村庄在八月半前后还请木偶戏班来演神戏。有些村子在宗祠门坪，有些村子则在大土楼外，搭个戏台，大家集资请个戏班子来演出。开场那天要摆神坛，人们焚香祭拜，木偶戏班则要开演折子戏。土楼客家人过中秋节之所以如此隆重，民俗文化活动也较多，主要是因那时候是秋收之后，寓意庆祝丰收。

■ Mid-Autumn Festival Reunions

The fifteenth day of the eighth lunar month is the Mid-Autumn Festival not only in China but also in some of its Asian neighbouring countries.

This day is the most important festival for the Hakka people after the summer harvest. During this time, the quiet period of the farmers has begun and the autumn festival has ended. It is a chance for family reunion. As such, apart from preparing moon cakes, the Hakka people also prepare the fruits, sweets, foods and wine to worship the moon. Like many other festivals, dinner is very important and the table is often covered in an array of dishes. A saying in Chinese explains that the first day of the lunar New Year is celebrated at breakfast, the Dragon Boat Festival is celebrated at lunch and the festivals in the seventh and eighth month are celebrated at dinner.

After a fulfilling dinner, a significant ritual is for all members of the family, young or old, to gather in the courtyard or by the main entrance. There will be traditional big square tables which will each have a large moon cake, grapefruit, candy and so on placed on top, although no alcohol will be present. An incense burner filled with rice will be placed facing where the moon rises. Every family will sit together at a table to enjoy the food while admiring the moon.

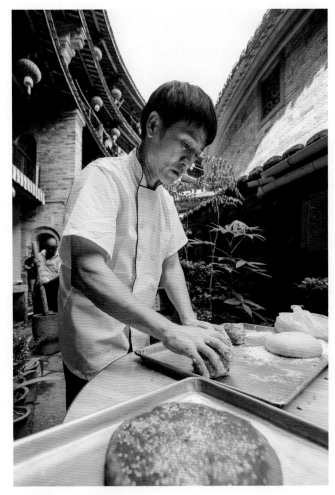

◎ 做月饼。（李艺爽 摄 ）
Making mooncakes. (Photo by Li Yishuang)

In some villages, stages may be set up for performances. The locals will all contribute to a fund so that they can invite a puppet theatre troupe. Respects will be paid and incense burnt before the troupe can begin their show. The reason why the Hakka people place such importance on the Mid-Autumn Festival is because it is the post-harvest celebration where they express their gratitude.

■ 登高祈福重阳节

农历九月初九是中国传统节日重阳节。土楼客家人称之为九月节，有的地方俗称兜尾节，意为一年最后一个重要节日，所以过得特别隆重。

与一些地方传统的重阳节登高祈福、游赏秋菊、佩插茱萸等习俗有所不同，土楼客家人重阳节最重要的活动是拜神祭祖，饮宴求寿。因为这个节日就在中秋节后不到一个月，人们仍处农闲，庆祝丰收余音未了，喜悦依然。所以，重阳节那天，人们除了在土楼外对着天摆上祭品祭拜天神、先祖外，还要到村庄周边神庙、神坛祭拜各方神圣。

土楼客家人重阳祀神祭祖，其实与中秋祭月一样，寓庆祝丰收，感谢天神、祖先恩德之意。如今，重阳节已被国家有关部门定为敬老节或老人节，增加了敬老新俗，正好契合了土楼客家人饮宴求寿之寓意。

■ The Double Ninth Festival

The ninth day of the ninth lunar month is the Double Ninth Festival, the last important holiday of the year so it is particularly grand.

Unlike other places where the practice of climbing mountains for luck or viewing autumn chrysanthemums is common, the Tulou Hakka people emphasise paying respects to their ancestors and the gods. Because the festival is not long after the Mid-Autumn Festival, people are still taking it easy from working in the fields. The celebrations of harvest have not yet ended and there is still much joy from the festivities. Therefore, on the day of the Double Ninth Festival, in addition to worshiping the gods and ancestors, people will also go to the temples.

Similar to the Mid-Autumn Festival, the Hakka people will give thanks for the harvest and ask for blessings. Nowadays, the festival is seen as a day for the elderly, reflecting the importance in Chinese culture to respect your elders. Just as well, it coincides with the Tulou people's feast for longevity.

© 重阳秋意浓。（冯木波 摄）
Beautiful autumn sight in the Double Ninth Festival. (Photo by Feng Mubo)

■ 土楼民俗做大福

做大福是土楼民间为了报答保生大帝恩德举办的一个特色民俗活动。每年的重阳节后，南靖、永定的土楼人都会举办隆重的做大福习俗，大家敬神演戏，以谢神灵。漳州南靖云水谣做大福习俗已有三百多年历史。节日期间，云水谣到处张灯结彩，村里请来戏班或木偶剧团，古老的村落响起锣鼓声、乐器声、鞭炮声、大人孩子的欢呼声，村里的居民和游客们都沉浸在热闹非凡的节日气氛当中。每年的农历十月二十三日，家家户户准备好鸡鸭鱼肉、水果、糍粑等供品，前往神庙虔诚祭拜，答谢神灵的同时，祈求神灵保佑。

■ Tulou Customs – Zuo Dafu

Zuo Dafu is a folk activity organised by the Tulou people for peace and prosperity. After the annual Double Ninth Festival, the people of the Yongding and Nanjing Tulou will hold a large banquet with performances and give thanks for the year's blessings. In Yunshuiyao, Nanjing, Zhangzhou, the custom of Zuo Dafu has been around for over 300 years. On that date, lights can be seen everywhere and the village is full of the echoes of drumming, musical instruments, firecrackers and the cheers of adults and children. Puppet theatre troupes are also invited while tourists and locals alike immerse themselves in the lively celebrations. Annually, on the twenty-third day of the tenth lunar month, every household will prepare a range of meats, seafood and fruits to take to the temples as offerings where they show their gratitude.

◎ 场面壮观的做大福。（陈军 摄）
A grand scene of Zuo Dafu. (Photo by Chen Jun)

◎ 南靖做大福时的狮子舞。（冯木波 摄 ）
Lion dance during Zuo Dafu in Nanjing. (Photo by Feng Mubo)

在距离南靖河坑土楼群约2千米的石桥村，是省级历史文化名村，该村每年都会在春季和冬季举办一次做大福，称为"春福"和"冬福"。该村的迎神活动也是别具特色，每到迎神当天，先从供奉保生大帝、圣王公、民主公王的水尾庵，把神像请进神轿抬回公王庙。迎神队伍浩浩荡荡、蔚为壮观，鼓乐齐鸣，鞭炮声、火铳声此起彼伏。做大福期间，村里会邀请戏班在公王庙前连续演戏三天。

About two kilometres away from Nanjing Hekeng Tulou Cluster is Shiqiao Village. It is a provincial-level historical and cultural village. Every year, the village will host a Zuo Dafu in spring and winter. The village's way for celebrating is also unique. On the day, the gods will be welcomed with the sounds of drumming and firecrackers as they are enshrined in the Gongwang Temple. During the Zuo Dafu period, the village will invite troupes to perform for three consecutive days in front of the Gongwang Temple.

永定土楼做大福，是永定湖坑镇李姓每三年举办一次的民俗活动，做大福的日期定在重阳节后（农历九月初九至十六）。从九月初十开始，人人斋戒五日，家家食素。农历九月十一辰牌时分，各村的"公王"相继到永定湖坑集镇西南边的"马额宫"前汇集。九时许，三声铳响之后，各路"公王"依次起轿上路，前往设在湖坑镇西片村中心坝的大福场。众"公王"到了神台后，人们便开始上供。

At Hukeng Town, Yongding, Zuo Dafu is an occasion that only happens once every three years. The date will always be after the Double Ninth Festival (usually between the ninth to sixteenth day of the ninth lunar month). From the tenth day of the ninth lunar month, everyone will practice vegetarianism for five days. On the eleventh day, every village will bring their respective Gong Wang idols to Ma'e Temple which is located in the southwest of Hukeng Town. At nine o'clock, after three directive sounds, the idols of each village will be carried via sedan to the site for Zuo Dafu. After the idols have arrived at the table where they will be placed, people will bring their offerings.

◎ 湖坑土楼做大福。（胡家新 摄 ）
Zuo Dafu at Hukeng Tulou Cluster. (Photo by Hu Jiaxin)

◎ 祈颂"风调雨顺，五谷丰登"。（胡家新 摄 ）

Praying for a good harvest and better living. (Photo by Hu Jiaxin)

　　直到农历九月十五一大早，从永定坎市迎来"保生大帝"，迎神路上，喇叭、唢呐、大鼓、锣钹，吹打不停。"保生大帝"一到大福场，顿时鞭炮声、炮铳声此起彼伏，震耳欲聋。各村现场杀猪行荤腥之祭，大福场上摆满了桌子，供桌上鸡鸭鱼肉、糖果、水果等贡品琳琅满目、应有尽有。九月十一到十五，大福场夜夜都有大班戏、木偶戏、电影、吹唱等。如今，做大福这种古老风俗的内涵也在逐渐发生变化，除了祈颂"风调雨顺，五谷丰登"，表达对美好生活的向往之外，还赋予了加强乡亲联谊、鼓励勤劳致富、吸引海外游子回乡寻根的意义。

Until the early morning on the fifteenth day, the idol for life will be greeted by the non-stop sound of horns, cymbals, and drums. As soon as the idol arrives, the deafening sounds of firecrackers will ring towards the people's ears. The offerings table will be covered in various meats, candies and fruits. From the eleventh until the fifteenth, there will be many activities to partake in such as movies, puppet shows and choirs. Nowadays, the ancient customs of Zuo Dafu have gradually changed. In addition to praying for a good harvest and better living, there are also meanings for strengthening the friendship between villagers, encouraging hard work, prosperity and the hopes that those working overseas will return back to their hometowns.

■ 土楼弥月礼俗

小孩出生满30天，便可以举行弥月礼，具体日子也要选择吉日，可以提前两三天，但是不能推后。因为这是婴儿第一次出门见世面，所以，弥月礼也是土楼人家中一次隆重的礼仪。弥月礼仪式主要有剃胎发、敬神、喊鹞婆、报丁、开斋等。

弥月礼当天一大早，婴儿的祖母或者外祖母会把婴儿抱着，准备给婴儿剃满月头，也称剃胎发。剃头时，因为婴儿的囟门还未闭合，所以只留下囟门的头发，起到保护之用。剃完头以后，便给婴儿换上新衣新帽新袜。然后由爷爷或者奶奶抱着到土楼里面的厅堂里，摆上供品，点燃香烛，祭拜神明。祭拜神明以后，婴儿的名单会按照辈分贴在厅堂的左墙壁上。

贴完名单，祖母或者"好命"的老人便会抱着婴儿从楼内走到楼外，或跑一跑，一边朝天上轻轻地举起婴儿，一边高喊："鹞婆！鹞婆！"客家话"鹞婆"即老鹰，土楼人家希望婴儿将来能够像老鹰一样雄健、一样自由翱翔。

喊过鹞婆后，婴儿的父亲便会挑着五牲祭品到宗祠祭告祖宗，把婴儿的名字写在一张红纸上，贴在祠堂的左边墙上，这个仪式叫"报丁"。

中午喜宴进行到一半的时候，主家会给婴儿举行隆重的开斋仪式。开斋人一般为知书达礼、德高望重的长辈，有的地方也由新生儿的外祖父或祖父主持。开斋前，开斋人要先用温水洗脸、洗手、净身，然后一边象征性地把备好的葱、豆腐、红圆子、鸡、鱼等食物碰一下婴儿的嘴唇，一边说一些吉利的话，大都是祝新生儿聪明伶俐、大富大贵、鲤鱼跳龙门等祝福语。开斋礼毕，主人会抱着婴儿分别敬酒，亲朋好友会把准备好的红包放在婴儿身上或开斋盛菜的大盘子上；散席后，主家要酌情回礼。

虽然各个土楼群的弥月礼形式不尽相同，但是大家的心愿都是一样的，寄托了长辈的殷切希望和美好的祝愿。

◎ 给婴儿开斋。（王福平 摄）
Breaking the fast.
(Photo by Wang Fuping)

◎ 给婴儿红包。（王福平 摄）
Presented with red envelops.
(Photo by Wang Fuping)

◎ 抱婴儿敬酒。（王福平 摄）
Holding the baby for a toast.
(Photo by Wang Fuping)

■ Celebrating Newborns in the Tulou

Once a newborn reaches the 30-day mark from their birth, there is a celebratory ceremony. The event must be done on an auspicious day. It can be done two or three days in advance, but cannot be later than the thirtieth day. Because this is the first time the baby will have been outside after the one month confinement period, the ceremony is a big affair. Customs include shaving the infant's hair and paying respect to the gods.

On the morning of the ceremony, the infant's maternal or paternal grandmother will caress the baby as their hair is shaved off. Because the baby's skull has not fully developed, a patch of hair is left for its protection. Once the baby has received his haircut, he is put into new clothing, a hat and stockings. After which, the baby is held by a grandparent inside the Tulou's main hall, offerings are given and incense sticks are lit as they pray to the gods. Next, the baby's name will be etched onto the left wall in the hall, in accordance with seniority.

After his name is listed, the grandmother, or an elderly with great fortune, will carry the baby outside. Gently lifting the child towards the sky, they will shout out "eagle" in the Hakka dialect several times in hope that the baby will be as free and magnificent as an eagle.

Once this has been done, the father will pick five sacrificial items for the ancestors, and write the child's name on a red piece of paper which will be attached to the left wall.

About halfway through the afternoon celebrations, the infant's immediate family will hold a ceremony for breaking the fast. The host is usually a respected elder of the family, although in some places it may be the grandfather. Before they begin, the host must wash his face and hands with warm water to cleanse the body. Then, they will symbolically hold the prepared onion, tofu, chicken and fish to the infant's lips while saying auspicious words. The idea is to bless the newborn to be smart and have good fortune. Once complete, the host will hold the baby up for a toast before relatives present the baby with red envelopes.

Although the way the event is held varies from each Tulou, everyone's wishes and intents are the same. They pass on the hopes and wishes from the elders to the newborn child.

■ 土楼婚嫁礼俗

旧时土楼人家的婚嫁大都也是遵循父母之命、媒妁之言。新中国成立以后，随着时代发展，男女青年才开始时兴相亲。男青年可以在媒人或者介绍人的陪同下到女方家，若女方父母亲对男青年满意，便会叫女青年出来见面。期间，男青年会给女青年一个"红包"作为见面礼，有的地方如果钱的金额是双数则表示男青年相中女青年，如果是单数则表示没有相中；有的地方如果红包的金额多则表示满意，红包少则不满意。而女青年如果对男青年有意也会有所表示，否则表示不愿意。当然，地域不同，表达方式也会有所区别。

男女双方如果觉得满意，表示这桩婚姻基本上可以确定了。接下来便有一套婚嫁过程，大致有合八字、选日子、起嫁、送嫁、迎亲、拜堂、宴请、洞房发烛、回娘家等。

女青年出嫁前一天，女方准备酒菜，一来宴请亲戚和送嫁的人，二来也是吃一顿团圆饭。迎亲之日，新娘往往会因为舍不得离开父母而流下眼泪，这也是土楼人家所说的"哭嫁"。长辈除了跟新娘说一些吉祥祝福语以外，还会叮嘱新娘到男方家后要孝敬公婆、勤俭持家、相夫教子等等。这也是中华民族"入孝""出悌"文化的传承。

◎ 土楼新娘。（王福平 摄）

A Tulou bride. (Photo by Wang Fuping)

■ Wedding Customs in the Tulou

In the old days, most marriages were arranged by parents or at the words of the matchmaker. Now, blind dates are more common and young males will go to the female's house while accompanied by their mutual introducer. If the female's parents are satisfied with the young man, they will ask their daughter to come out to meet him. At this time, the young man will give the young woman a red envelope with some money wrapped in as a gift upon meeting the first time. In some places, the amount of money within the envelopes can be symbolic. If it is an even number, it means the male is interested but if it is an odd number, then there will be no further progression in the relationship. In other places, if the amount of the money is large, it is satisfactory; if it is small, then it is not. If the females are willing, they are able to openly express their interests.

If both parties are happy, the prospects of marriage can be determined. Next there is a process where specific auspicious dates are chosen for when the Chinese wedding traditions take place. These include the date of the wedding, the day the girl leaves home for her new family, the banquet and the return back to the girl's home.

The day before the female is married, her family will prepare food and wine. Relatives of the bride will be invited over for two reasons: a reunion dinner, and to send the bride off. On the day of the wedding, the bride often cries because she is reluctant to leave her parents. Elders will pass on their blessings while reminding the bride to be a filial daughter-in-law and a loving wife.

◎ 土楼新郎。（王福平 摄 ）
A Tulou bridegroom. (Photo by Wang Fuping)

© 迎新娘入门。（赖永生 摄）
Bringing the bride home. (Photo by Lai Yongsheng)

迎亲吉时，男方便会请鼓乐队用红轿或者花轿迎接新娘。新娘出嫁时由伴娘陪去新郎家。新娘坐着花轿，鼓乐队伍吹吹打打，迎亲队伍热热闹闹，喜气洋洋。到夫家门前时，会由一位有福气的老阿婆或"好命"的妇女将新娘牵出花轿，新郎新娘在鞭炮声中跨过男家的大门，进入厅堂以后，在主持人的引导下拜菩萨、拜天地、拜父母长辈，然后夫妻对拜。拜过堂后，新郎新娘共同步入洞房。

婚宴后，洞房要点燃蜡烛，俗称"发烛"，"发烛"结束后放鞭炮。而此时，大家也酒足饭饱，自然少不了到新郎新娘的洞房取闹一番，欢快的闹洞房给新婚人家带来许多乐趣和无尽的祝福。

婚后第二天早上，新娘要一一问候家中长辈，并向公婆敬茶。第三天，新郎新娘要一同回娘家，俗称"回门"。吃完午饭，双方再返回新郎家。完成这些礼俗以后，婚礼才算正式结束。

改革开放以来，土楼人家的思想日益开放，更多青年男女选择自由恋爱了。婚礼也不再拘泥于传统，或多或少地融入了现代元素。有的土楼婚礼还把传统婚礼和西方婚礼相融合，犹如"中西合璧"的土楼一样，显示出其文化包容性和多样性。

When welcoming his bride, the groom will have a drum band ready to greet the bride and her bridesmaids. The bride arrives on a red sedan chair to the beat of the drums. The atmosphere is warm and happy. Once the bride and her party have arrived at the groom's house, a woman who is meant to bring fortune, will help the bride off her sedan chair. The bride and groom cross the threshold into his house while firecrackers go off in the background. Upon entering a hall, a host will guide them in paying their respects to Buddha, the heavens and earth, parents and elders before bowing to each other. Afterwards, the bride and groom must walk in sync to enter the bridal room.

After dinner, there will be candles lit inside followed by more firecrackers going off outside. At this point, everyone will be full of food and wine so naturally, they will play some interesting jokes on the couple and make lots of noise in the room. This is a tradition that is intended to bring lots of fun and endless blessings to the newly-weds.

The next morning, the bride will greet the elders and the in-laws with tea. On the third day, the bride and groom will return to the bride's home together. After having lunch, they must then go back to the groom's house. Once the rituals are completed, the wedding is officially over.

Because of modernisation, the thoughts of the Tulou people have become more open. Weddings are no longer limited by traditions, and have adopted more of a western vibe. Some Tulou weddings now have influences from both traditional and modern etiquettes, a bit like the Chinese Tulou with hints of Western designs. Both retain traditional customs while incorporating modern elements.

◎ 做芋子包。（李艺爽 摄 ）
Making taro cakes. (Photo by Li Yishuang)

土楼故里品美食

　　土楼地处东南山区，气候温和，雨量充沛，盛产水稻，也种植其他五谷杂粮。一般水源较好的田地用来种水稻，有单季稻，也有双季稻；山地、旱地则种一些地瓜、芋头、小米、粟米、高粱、小麦等。土楼人家勤劳节俭、心灵手巧，他们可以把糯米或大米做成形状各异、五花八门、美味可口的粄，如发粄、软粄、硬粄、水粄、禾米粄、千层粄、猪肠粄、老鼠粄、鹞婆粄、状元糕、糍粑、粽子等等。粄是用大米磨粉制皮，用豆干、咸菜、萝卜、瘦肉、鲜笋等制成馅，包成各种形状的类似饺子的食物，是土楼人的一款地道主食。大米和麦面还可以制作成各种粉条面条，如大粉干、米粉、线面、手工面、鸡肠面等等。地瓜和芋头等杂粮掺入面粉或者薯粉，可以做成大肉圆、芋子粄、芋子包、地瓜粄等等。

The Tastes of the Tulou

Fujian Tulou are found in mountainous areas in the southeast of China, where the climate is mild and there is plenty of rain, perfect for the cultivation of grains. Well irrigated paddies are used to grow rice, whereas harsher land is used to grow sweet potatoes, taro, millet, corn, sorghum and wheat. The Tulou people are innovative and creative; using rice, they have created a special delicious range of rice cakes called *ban* in the dialect. *Ban* has fillings such as dried bean curd, radish, pickled vegetables, meat or bamboo shoot, and is a staple food in Tulou. They also integrate sweet potatoes and taro into these recipes, creating flavoured rice cakes and buns. The Tulou people also use rice and wheat to make a variety of noodles, including wheat noodles, rice vermicelli and misua.

◎ 风干的美食。（冯木波 摄 ）
Special dry food.
(Photo by Feng Mubo)

　　土楼客家的肉食多以自家原生态养殖的鸡、鸭、猪、牛、羊等为主。经过蒸、煮、焖、炒、炖、煲、煨、烤等烹饪形式，配以当地的米酒、荷叶、姜等配料，做成酒娘鸡、盐煨鸡、荷叶鸡、盐水鸭、客家姜母鸭、仔姜炒鸭公仔、菜头焖家鸭、芋焖家鸭、酒娘荷包蛋、菜干扣肉、乳蒸猪肉、巴浪干蒸猪肉、萝卜焖牛腩、雪豆炒腊肉、芋子焖牛肉、红菇焖玉兔、酒香龙骨、粉蒸龙骨等色香味俱全的独特菜肴。

　　除了自家养殖的各种牲畜以外，还有野生野长在崇山峻岭、深涧河流的山珍野味，如野猪、山羊、黄猄、野兔、蛇类、石鳞、田鸡、河鱼、河虾、田螺等；以及从山中土壤里冒出的竹笋、山蕨、灵芝、香菇、红菇等；山珍野味以清蒸、炸、煮、焖、煎、炒、炖、煲、煨、烤等烹饪形式，做出家喻户晓的爆炒野猪肉、蒜香石鳞、酸菜肉末煮棘心、酸菜肉丝炒山蕨、金钱莲蒸石鳞、党参枸杞蒸野兔、老母鸡汤炆春笋、黄瓜炒膳片、韭菜炒河虾、豆腐炖红鲤、酒娘焖黄鸭子、炒石螺子等美味佳肴，还有各种香甜可口的灵芝汤、菇汤等等。

Meat in Tulou comes predominantly from the animals they raise. Most Tulou have chickens, ducks, pigs, cattle and sheep. Cooked in many ways, including, but not limited to, steaming, boiling, frying, stewing and braising, and infused with Chinese spices such as local rice wine, bay leaves and ginger, the results are mouth-watering. Famous dishes include salted chicken, Hakka ginger chicken, taro duck, braised pork with preserved vegetables, fermented rice and egg, clay pot duck, braised beef and turnip, snow peas stir fried with preserved meat, and the list goes on.

In addition to the livestock raised by the residents, there are also wild animals that live in the mountains, including mountain goats, boars, snakes, frogs, hares, fish and prawn. Bamboo shoots, mushrooms and mountain ferns also enhance the flavour of many dishes, bringing a strong earthy flavour to dishes such as stir-fried boar, *dangshen* hare and mushroom soups.

◎ 牛肉丸。（赖永生 摄 ）

Beef balls. (Photo by Lai Yongsheng)

◎ 糍粑。（赖永生 摄 ）

Glutinous rice cakes. (Photo by Lai Yongsheng)

◎ 芋饺。（赖永生 摄 ）

Taro dumplings. (Photo by Lai Yongsheng)

　　土楼人家长期生活在大山深处，特别擅长利用大自然的一些草药，用来医治病痛。有的则根据时节天气，把不同的草药辅以肉类烹饪成可口的炖汤，又起到滋阴降火、清凉解毒、祛风除湿、舒筋活络、通经活脉、清肝明目、壮腰补肾、养颜益气、延年益寿等养生保健的效果。其中有雄鸡酒宝、三七炖鸭胗、巴戟枸杞牛鞭煲、牛奶子根炖鸭块、金银花炖龙骨、灯芯草蒸猪心、香藤根炖家鸭、艾根炖老母鸡、苦斋煲大肠、乌豆艾根煲猪尾、七叶布荆炖老母鸡、益母草煮蛋、狗贴耳焖狗肉、羊耳三点炖玉兔、黄丝鸡鸢炖排骨、天麻炖猪脑、茯苓生地蒸排骨、溪黄鱼头汤等药食同源的美味炖汤。

　　在土楼人家的门前屋后，或者山脚溪边，只要有空地，都会有勤劳的农家妇女种瓜种菜，所以，一年四季瓜果蔬菜，翠绿诱人。这些瓜果蔬菜通过猛火快炒以及煮、漉、热拌、凉拌等烹饪方式做成香气扑鼻的蒜香血蕨、酿豆腐、酸菜煮芋卵、酿苦瓜、油浇地瓜叶、扒茄羹嫩茄子、油泼南瓜花、酸菜焖四季豆、清焖紫藤菜等。

　　吃不完的一些蔬菜、豆子，经过晾晒、腌制，采用上千年的传统工艺和独特配方，制作成色香味俱全的客家酸菜、菜干、豆干、芋荷干、笋干、蕨干等等，成为土楼人家中必备的家常菜，也成为深受大众喜爱的店家特色菜。

The Tulou people have lived in mountainous area for many generations now. Over the years, they have accumulated a wealth of knowledge regarding medicinal herbs. Depending on the season, different herbs are added to stews, both enhancing their flavour and providing health benefits. There are countless stews using these herbs that address different ailments according to traditional Chinese medicinal studies.

The Tulou people make the most of their space. Any empty land is promptly converted to a vegetable patch, which provides food all year round. As a key food group, there are many vegetable dishes in Tulou cuisine, making use of all sorts of vegetables—beans, eggplants, bitter melon, wisteria and otherwise.

Vegetables not immediately consumed are dried, preserved and marinated. Using traditional techniques developed over centuries, Hakka pickled vegetables and preserved vegetables are made. These have become an integral part of Tulou cuisine and are always a crowd favourite.

◎ 上：梅菜扣肉。 下：牛肉片。（舌尖之福 供图）
Above: Steamed pork with preserved vegetable.
Bottom: Sliled beef. (Courtesy of Shejian Style)

土楼民间艺术

千百年来，客家地区广泛流传着许多独具地方特色的民间技艺，其中，在土楼流传的主要有客家山歌、客家十番音乐、树叶吹奏、木偶戏等。

Tulou Traditional Arts

The Hakka people boast a rich, unique history, of which art is a key part. They embrace many diverse forms of art, including folk songs, special local music and puppet shows.

■ 客家山歌

客家山歌用客家方言吟唱，内容广泛，即兴创作，现编现唱，语言朴素生动，旋律非常优美，富有浓郁的山村生活气息。

前些年，在永定洪坑土楼群，经常可以看到一位老年人，一边演唱客家山歌《八月十五看月光》，一边神情专注地指导几个年轻男女。他就是曾经为毛主席、周总理等党和国家领导人演唱过客家山歌的"山歌大王"李天生。他从小就在客家农村接受客家山歌的熏陶，几十年来对山歌有着很深的感情，他那音域宽广、音色明亮、民间风格浓郁的歌声，深受广大观众的欢迎，他还能一人表演男女声山歌对唱。经过李天生的传帮带，当地已经培养出了很多优秀的山歌人才。

在南靖田螺坑土楼群，也有一群以王旭辉、张巧儿为主的客家山歌传唱者。王旭辉还是南靖县田螺坑客家山歌第二十一代传承人。他们为了客家山歌的传承和发展做出了一定的贡献。这些声调悠扬、甜美的客家山歌，常常飘荡于土楼村落的田野、林间、溪畔，回响在每一座土楼里，饱含着深情，凝聚着希望。

◎ 李天生和他的学生们。（王福平 摄 ）

Li Tiansheng and his students. (Photo by Wang Fuping)

■ Hakka Folk Songs

Hakka folk songs are sung in the Hakka dialect and reflect the thoughts and feelings of the people singing. The lyrics are moving and the melodies beautiful.

A few years ago, near the Hongkeng Tulou Cluster in Yongding , an elderly man was often seen singing "The moon on August 15th", a Hakka folk song, whilst teaching younger folk to dance. He is none other than "king of folk songs" Li Tiansheng, who has performed for national leaders including Chairman Mao and Premier Zhou. Having grown up in a Hakka village, he has always felt a deep connection to the folk songs he sings. His lively music, sung in a bright folk style is always well received, and he is so well versed in these songs that he can perform a male-female duet by himself! Due to the tutelage of Li Tiansheng, the local area has produced many fantastic folk musicians.

In another Tulou community, the Tianluokeng Tulou Cluster in Nanjing, Wang Xuhui and Zhang Qiaoer manage a folk song singing group. Wang Xuhui is the 21st generation of inheritors of the folk songs and has made significant contributions to bringing attention to Hakka folk songs. These wonderful songs can be heard through the mountains, fields and forests near Tulou villages as well as the Tulou themselves, filling these places with joy and hope.

■ 客家十番音乐

　　客家十番音乐是一种民间音乐，用二胡、扬琴、琵琶、竹笛、唢呐等十余件乐器演奏，有"喇叭戏""文武场""锣鼓吹"等几种演奏形式。十番音乐的乐队一般由五到七人组成，多的时候也有十到几十人不等。其乐曲除了描绘大自然及客家人生活习俗情趣以外，还吸收了历代戏曲剧种中的曲段、唱段和曲艺作品等。那种由清脆的鼓乐声、悦耳的琵琶声、清亮的二胡音等组成的各种乐器声，在古老的土楼村落显得那么悠扬动听。

◎ 一支老人组成的十番乐队。（赖永生 摄）
A Shifan music band composed of old players. (Photo by Lai Yongsheng)

■ Hakka Shifan Music

Hakka Shifan music is a specific type of folk music, played using traditional instruments including the erhu, dulcimer, pipa and bamboo flute. Shifan music bands are generally composed of five to seven people, although larger groups of even dozens of people have performed together in past. Other than original works, Shifan music has also absorbed passages of music and song from the past. The steady drumming, relaxing humming and clear erhu melody combine into graceful music that washes over the Tulou.

■ 树叶吹奏

在永定土楼，除了经常响起客家山歌以外，还时常能够听到用树叶吹奏的美妙声音。客家土楼艺人田间劳作之余，信手拈来一片树叶，就可以吹出优美的乐章。民间树叶吹奏由来已久。在永定，有一个人把树叶吹奏这门技艺发扬光大，甚至别出心裁地加工创新，从吹树叶到吹竹叶、吹花瓣、吹绸布，甚至吹塑料片、吹易拉罐、吹牛皮等等，他就是曾荣获"上海大世界吉尼斯纪录"和中央电视台"挑战英雄"的阮宏昌。他从小学吹树叶，几十年来，经过不断探索吹奏技艺与吹奏材料的创新，他吹奏出的各种音乐悠扬动听，还被国内外游客和群众誉为土楼"神吹手"。

■ Music in Leaves

At the Tulou in Yongding, a fascinating form of music has taken roots. Along with the folk songs, people play music using leaves. Tulou people have mastered the art of playing tunes by merely blowing into leaves in a certain way. One person has even transferred this skill to other materials, playing melodies on petals, fabric and even plastic and leather. He holds a Guinness world record and an award from China Central Television. His name is Ruan Hongchang and he has been blowing leaves (and other materials) since his elementary school days. His devotion to his craft has been recognised both locally and internationally and videos of him can be found online.

◎ 教游客吹树叶。（王福平 摄）
Ruan Hongchang is teaching visitors to play music with leaves. (Photo by Wang Fuping)

◎ 正在表演的李福渊。（王福平 摄）

A live performance of Li Fuyuan. (Photo by Wang Fuping)

■ 土楼绝技王

在永定土楼，经常跟李天生、阮宏昌一起表演的还有"土楼绝技王"李福渊，他出身于一个充满音乐氛围的竹匠家庭，经过数十年的苦练，如今一个人便可以同时使用多种乐器演奏乐曲，他充分利用身体各个器官，不断地给自己增加难度，同时可以吹、拉、弹、奏、打，挑战演奏乐器的极限，每一场演出都会引起轰动，几乎全国的卫视都邀请他录过节目。由于他这种罕见的民间技艺，2005年他被文化部授予"中国民间绝艺王"的称号。

■ The King of Chinese Folk Music

Often performing together with Li Tiansheng and Ruan Hongchang is Li Fuyuan. After spending a childhood in a home filled with music, he spent decades practicing his artistry. Now, he can simultaneously play multiple instruments, effectively playing as a one-man band. It is an incredible sight to see, and practically every broadcasting company in China has requested a show from him at some point. Given his immense talent, he has been dubbed the "king of Chinese folk music".

■ 木偶戏

不论是在永定土楼，还是南靖土楼，都经常可以看到木偶戏上演。木偶戏又称傀儡戏，闽南地区也称之为提线木偶戏。土楼山区经过悠久的历史传承，形成了一种适合农村老年人口味和欣赏习惯的民间技艺。每尊木偶身上设置8至16条提线，较复杂的表演多至36条线。线分若干组，木偶的一举一动，全凭演员用五指操纵完成，不仅能体现人戏的唱、念、做、打，还能表现出各种栩栩如生的表情。

南靖提线木偶戏传承人魏敢相还是市级代表性传承人，以他和剧团兴衰为主线拍摄的《戏班》电视专题片在中央电视台多个频道播放，反响强烈。出生在南靖和贵楼的简立真也是南靖提线木偶戏传承人，她把地方戏曲歌仔戏(芗剧)唱腔、口白、乐队弹琴、打锣、打鼓等各种技巧融入木偶戏表演中，为传承民间传统木偶表演艺术做出积极贡献。

◎ 提线木偶。（冯木波 摄）
String puppets. (Photo by Feng Mubo)

■ Traditional Puppetry

In all Tulou communities, puppet shows are often held. This is an art that has evolved over many years, and is particularly popular with older folks, where puppeteers masterfully manipulate the puppets to tell stories. Each puppet has 8 to 16 strings, or up to 36 strings for some more complex performances. The strings are divided into several groups, all controlled by the hands of the puppeteers.

Wei Ganxiang is a key member of the Nanjing Tulou puppeteers. He and his troupe filmed a show titled "A Theatrical Troupe", which has since been shown on TV across the country. Another performer, Jian Lizhen, has incorporated singing, drumming and other musical accompaniment into her shows. The current generation of puppeteers bring new and exciting innovations to this art, and so traditional puppetry continues to grow.

◎ 教游客表演提线木偶。（冯木波 摄）
Teaching a visitor to manipulate the puppet. (Photo by Feng Mubo)

■ 竹马戏

竹马戏始于唐，又叫马艺、马灯、竹马灯。竹马戏的道具是用竹篾扎成马的形状，用多种颜色的纸糊制而成。演出时，一般由8人、9人、12人、16人组成演出阵容，这些穿着戏服的少男少女，分别把一只竹马挂在齐腰处，看上去，几位小演员就像骑在马上，加上骑马的动作，可以说惟妙惟肖。他（她）们被打扮成昭君、番王、小生、婢女等人物，在鼓、锣、钹等乐器的伴奏下，以围场、南蛇游、四柱穿、叠马等多种队形进行表演。看似一板一眼简单的节奏，加上男女少年演员的脸部表情和各种有趣的动作，使得整个表演生动活泼。表演后，演员们站成一圈，在乐队声中，每人唱一段具有当地特色的南音，旋律细腻缠绵，有着浓厚的乡土风味。他们走村串社，挨家挨户表演，祈求合境平安，风调雨顺。活动全部结束以后，据说要焚烧竹马，把竹马送归天庭。

如今，竹马戏列入福建省第一批非物质文化遗产，在南靖土楼的重大节日和大型活动中，都能看到竹马戏的表演。

◎ 竹马戏大师和他的学生们。（冯木波 摄）

A Zhuma Theatre master and his students. (Photo by Feng Mubo)

◎ 骑着竹马的小演员。（赖永生 摄）
Young players riding on paper horses. (Photo by Lai Yongsheng)

■ Bamboo Horse Theatre

Zhuma Theatre, which roughly translates to bamboo horse theatre, is a form of Tulou theatre which originated from the Tang Dynasty. The name comes from horses made of bamboo and colourful paper. The show usually involves a dozen or so performers, each of whom have a bamboo horse attached to their clothing, making them seem like they are riding horses. Their acting, along with supporting music and sound effects enthral audiences in riveting historic theatre. At the end of the show, the cast members stand in a circle, and each member sings a passage of a local folk song, adding to the authenticity of the experience. They parade through the Tulou village, bringing joy and praying for prosperity wherever they go. After it is all over, it is said that sometimes the bamboo horses will be cremated in a ritual that sends them to heaven.

Today, Zhuma Theatre is one of the first intangible cultural heritage items of Fujian Province, and can be seen in any major festival at Nanjing Tulou.

◎ 大鼓凉伞。（赖永生 摄）

Drum and Parasol Dance. (Photo by Lai Yongsheng)

■ 大鼓凉伞

　　大鼓凉伞是一种地方传统舞蹈，舞队人数一般为8至12对，也有的二三十对。表演时，一群身着武士古装的小伙子，胸挂小鼓，双手紧握鼓槌，在大鼓的引导下有节奏地敲打小鼓，并一边打鼓一边变换舞姿，动作矫健潇洒，极具阳刚之美。旁边的一群少女们身着小旦装，一边跳着形式多样的舞蹈，一边上下旋转舞动着造型特别的凉伞，舞蹈的步伐跟旋转凉伞的动作互相配合，节奏鲜明。在这群青年男女表演的队伍之中，有时还会出现一对动作滑稽、互相打俏的老头儿和老太太，显得诙谐搞笑，让人看后意犹未尽。

　　作为省级非物质文化遗产项目的大鼓凉伞，得到了较好的传承和创新。如今，在土楼人家逢年过节或喜庆活动时，常可一睹大鼓凉伞的风采。

■ Drum and Parasol Dance

Drum and Parasol Dance is a traditional Tulou dance involving drums, usually with eight to twelve pairs of dancers. During the performance, young men dress as warriors from the past, each with handheld drums. A large drum dictates the rhythm of the dance, which the men match with their own drums as they dance with a vigorous energy. Their partners, young women, dance elegantly with parasols. The spinning of the parasols and the skilful dancing is mesmerising. In the middle of all these young dancers is a single elderly couple, who dance playfully. Their presence adds a change of pace and some humour to the performance, creating a truly memorable experience.

This dance is also an intangible cultural heritage item of Fujian and will always be performed during traditional festivals and major events in the Tulou.

■ 四平锣鼓

四平锣鼓俗称粗锣鼓，在南靖流传了500多年。其主要特点是把一个民间戏剧节目通过锣鼓钹打击和唢呐吹奏表现出来。演奏时，一般由8个人组成一个四平锣鼓队，有时也会根据实际情况增加2至4人进行演奏，演奏曲调丰富，融合了本土曲调和外来曲调。锣的喤喤声、鼓的咚锵声、钹的伴奏声，以及唢呐或高或低的旋律声，各种曲调、音律紧密配合，节奏明快，旋律动听，深受老百姓的喜爱。

四平锣鼓乐常年伴随民间民俗活动，参加农村庙会、庆典等活动，深深扎根农村。自从成功申报为省级非物质文化遗产项目以后，得到了政府的宣传、重视和保护，这一传统的民间艺术也得到了更好的传承和发扬光大。

■ Siping Drums

Siping Drums is a drum performance that first came about 500 years ago in Nanjing. Utilising drums, gongs and cymbals, a Siping drum troupe usually has eight members, with additional 2 or 4 members and instruments sometimes. Although drums, cymbals and gongs are all loud instruments, they come together to create textured rhythms and strong melodies, drawing crowds of people to the show.

Siping Drums accompanies various traditional activities throughout the year and is an indispensable part of any celebration. Much like the Bamboo Horse Theatre and the Drum and Parasol Dance, Siping Drums has garnered more attention and fame since it was acknowledged as an intangible cultural heritage item of Fujian.

© 四平锣鼓。（吴智勇 摄）
Siping drums. (Photo by Wu Zhiyong)

◎ 玄天上帝巡游二宜楼。（胡家新 摄）
Celebration of Xuantian God in Eryilou. (Photo by Hu Jiaxin)

土楼多元信仰

　　土楼居民崇敬祖先、尊重自然、敬畏神灵，当地信仰的神祇众多，不仅有玉皇大帝、如来佛祖、观音菩萨，妈祖娘娘，还有"关帝""保生大帝""土地公""公王""伯公"等。

Religion in the Tulou

Tulou people are traditional in the ways they honour their ancestors and nature, always showing utmost respect. When it comes to religion, Tulou people are polytheists, not only worshiping the Jade Emperor, Buddha, Guanyin bodhisattva and Mazu (Goddess of the Sea) but also local Taoist gods such as Guandi (God of War) , Baosheng Dadi (God of Life), and Tudi Gong (God of Earth).

◎ 祭拜保生大帝。（王福平 摄）
Worship Baosheng Dadi (God of Life). (Photo by Wang Fuping)

◎ 梅林"妈祖节"。（冯木波 摄）
Celebration of Mazu's birthday in Meilin. (Photo by Feng Mubo)

20世纪初，南靖县和永定县许多当地人漂洋过海到香港、澳门、台湾及东南亚一带谋生，为保佑他们平安归来，南靖县和永定县许多村庄便建起了天后宫，供奉东南沿海民众信仰的"妈祖娘娘"。

永定洪坑土楼群也有一座建于清朝嘉庆年间的天后宫，每年农历三月二十三和九月二十三，洪坑村林姓人都要准备供品，举行隆重的祭拜仪式。如今，这座装饰华丽的天后宫成为世界文化遗产永定洪坑土楼之旅的重要一景。

南靖县梅林镇也会在每年的农历三月二十三举办土楼妈祖民俗文化节，这个民俗活动已经延续了300多年。活动当天，当地村民都要准备好鸡鸭鱼肉、糍粑和糖果等供品到妈祖天后宫烧香祈福。当地会组织一队人马抬着妈祖神像在鼓乐声、鞭炮声中巡游，一队人马舞龙舞狮，所到之处都会有村民摆上供品祭拜。四邻八方甚至海外的信众都会赶来参加这个民间盛会，共同庆祝"妈祖娘娘"的诞辰日。

◎ 洪坑村天后宫。（王福平 摄）
The Tianhou Temple in Hongkeng Village. (Photo by Wang Fuping)

At the beginning of the 20th century, many Tulou residents left for Hong Kong, Macau, Taiwan and other Southeast Asia countries to make a living. These voyages are believed to have been safeguarded by Mazu, and since then, Mazu has become a more prevalent deity in the Tulou community.

Located within the Hongkeng Tulou Cluster is a Tianhou temple, built during the Qing Dynasty and dedicated to Mazu. Every year, on March 23rd and September 23rd of the lunar calendar, locals prepare offerings of fruit and meat for Mazu. Today, this ornately decorated temple is an important stop in the Yongding Tulou for any tourist.

Meilin, a town in Nanjing County, also holds a festival in celebration of Mazu every March 23rd (lunar calendar), a tradition of more than three centuries. On the day, families offer precious chicken, duck, fish and other dishes at temples worshiping Mazu, where they burn incense and pray. The local council organises a team of people to parade a Mazu statue, announced by drums and firecrackers. Costumed lions and dragons also join the procession, drawing villagers and tourists from all over to celebrate Mazu's birthday.

◎ 妈祖过海。（胡家新 摄）
Parade a Mazu statue through water. (Photo by Hu Jiaxin)

土楼祖先崇拜

　　树不离根，水不离源，念祖追宗是中华民族的优良传统。客家先民历经种种磨难数次南迁，念祖思亲之情尤为浓烈。因此，在每一个土楼村落，几乎各姓宗族都有自己的宗祠，祠堂里供奉着祖先牌位，族人在此共同祭拜祖先，有时也在此共同商议族内重要事务。

　　土楼里每一个宗族都有自己的族谱，族谱里记载着族人繁衍、家族兴衰的历史，见证着一个家族的延续。土楼人把族谱视为家里最贵重的东西，时时用一个礼龛珍藏。

　　祭拜祖先、研修族谱，才能知道自己的根在哪里，才能永远记住自己的祖先。崇拜祖先，追根溯源，维系着土楼家族的凝聚力、向心力。

Ancestor Worship in the Tulou

Trees cannot grow without their roots. The Chinese keep the tradition of remembering and respecting their ancestors. People in the Tulou have strong emotional ties for their ancestors. There is an ancestral hall for almost every clan, where the tablets of the clan's ancestors are worshiped. It is believed that the ancestral hall is the habitat of the ancestors' souls. An ancestral hall is usually in a special place outside each Tulou.

Every clan at each Tulou has its own genealogy which records the family tree and historical moments. The genealogy is the witness to a clan's legacy and is thus held in high regard and value. It is a collection of a family's rituals and traditions. By paying respects to the ancestors and studying the genealogy, the legacy will forever live on and maintain the cohesiveness within the Tulou family.

　　春节祭祖是最隆重的。土楼人无论身在何处，离家多远，都要赶回土楼村里参加祭祖。大年三十，也就是除夕早饭后，凡是当年添了男丁的家庭都要派人到宗祠打扫卫生，然后在各楼的厅堂挂起祖宗画像。同族宗亲或挑或提着备好的三牲、香烛、鞭炮、元宝等祭品前往宗祠祭拜焚香。宗亲们兴高采烈聚在一起，一边祭拜祖宗，一边敲锣打鼓，一边燃放鞭炮。在宗祠祭拜以后，各楼再回到各自的厅堂吃年夜饭并拜祖先像。除夕之夜，全楼的宗亲便会聚集在厅堂守岁，楼里的老老少少欢聚一堂，喝茶聊天，迎接新年的到来。

　　大年初一上午，每座土楼的男男女女都会穿上新衣服，聚集到楼内的厅堂，由本楼德高望重的楼长主持在厅堂点燃香烛，在供桌上摆满供品，一起拜祖先像，楼长则讲述起祖宗的功德，向后辈宣讲本族或本楼的家风家训。礼仪结束，大家方才开始互相拜年，或到别的土楼串门拜年了。

　　客家地区，一般从除夕开始，都会在祠堂和楼内的厅堂点燃香烛，一直到元宵以后，祭祀周期才算结束，再恭恭敬敬地将祖宗的画像卷起悬挂起来，等待来年再用。

The worship ceremony at the Chinese Spring Festival is of the greatest importance. No matter where they live and how far away they are from the Tulou, all the descendants make their way home. After breakfast on the eve of the lunar New Year, every family with a baby boy born during the last year sends someone to clean the ancestral hall and hang the ancestral portraits in the family halls of each Tulou. Families of the same clan head for the ancestral hall and worship the ancestors with well-prepared beef, lamb and pork, incense candles, firecrackers, paper ingots and so on. People gather happily together, beat gongs and drums and set off firecrackers. After the worship ceremony in the ancestral hall, each family returns to their respective Tulou, has a grand New Year eve's dinner and lays offerings to the ancestral portraits in the family hall. The old and the young sit together, drink tea and chat joyfully to welcome the New Year.

On the morning of Chinese New Year's Day, everybody in every Tulou changes into new clothes and get together in the family hall of the building. A ceremony is hosted by a respected elder, in which the family members burn incense and candles, fill the altar with offerings and worship the ancestors together. The elder then speaks of the merits of the ancestors, as well as teaches the family traditions to the younger generations. When the ceremony is over, people undertake New Year visitations to wish each other well.

The Hakka people usually keep incense and candles burning in the ancestral halls and family halls from New Year's Eve until after the Lantern Festival, when the worship period ends. They respectfully roll up the ancestral portraits and store them carefully for reuse next year.

◎ 传统祭祖。（胡剑文 摄）

A traditional ancestor worship. (Photo by Hu Jianwen)

正月初五以后，土楼人家便开始上坟祭祖了，祭祖方式一般是先祭近祖再祭远祖。祭祀开基祖先或年代久远的上祖最为隆重。这时候，祭祖队伍不仅仅是本村，也有可能是外村的甚至更远的地方同姓同族的人，大家举着公祭的条幅，或抬或挑着供品，举着灯笼，鸣锣开道，浩浩荡荡。众人到了墓地之后先打扫墓地，再摆上供品，点燃香烛，大家先后有序，恭恭敬敬地祭拜祖先，此时，锣鼓喧天，烟花绽放、鞭炮响起，热闹非凡。祭拜仪式结束后，大家便一起吃饭喝酒，共商同宗同族的公益事业。

每年除了最重要的春祭以外，土楼人家还有清明祭祀以及七月节祭祀等。此外，还有规模较小的家祭。每逢农历初一十五、婚嫁生子或者外出经商求学，楼内的老人、妇女都要在厅堂或宗祠祭祀，一来提醒大家要时刻铭记祖先恩德，二来祈求祖先庇佑子孙后代。

土楼人崇敬祖先，通过各种祭祀活动，既传承了"慎终追远、报本返始"的传统美德，又起到了尊重长辈、团结宗亲、互相帮助的作用。土楼人家历经数百年繁衍生息，团结互助，靠的就是对祖先的敬仰！让遍布各地的土楼子孙都能够维系家族的团结，传承土楼的精神，守护血脉相连的家园。

After the fifth day of the first lunar month, people in Tulou visit their family graves to cherish the memory of their ancestors. Usually, people worship the younger ancestors first, followed by the worship of older ancestors. The ceremony to worship the oldest is the most significant. All relatives with the same surname come from other villages or even farther away to take part in the worship. They hold memorial banners, carry offerings, hold lanterns and beat gongs all the way to the grave. When arriving, they sweep the grave, place offerings on it and burn incense and candles. Everyone performs the worship ceremony in an orderly and respectful way. Then the gongs and drums are played loudly; fireworks bloom in the sky while firecrackers make a deafening sound. After the worship ceremony, the clan members always have a big dinner together, toast each other and discuss the public affairs of their clan.

Besides the most important worship ceremony during the Spring Festival, there are other worship ceremonies such as the Qingming Festival and Zhongyuan Festival. Smaller-scale worship ceremonies in each family are also frequently held. On the first and the fifteenth day of each lunar month, or when someone in Tulou is going to get married, give birth, do business or study outside the village, the elderly and females in this Tulou will perform worship ceremonies in the family hall or the ancestral hall. These ceremonies remind people in the Tulou of their ancestors' favor as they pray for the blessings of their ancestors to their descendants.

Through various worship activities, people in the Tulou inherit the virtues of remembering their history and origins, as well as respecting the elders, uniting the clans and helping each other. This helps keep the clans tightly knit for hundreds of years as they grow. No matter where the descendants are, they maintain family unity, inherit the spirit of the Tulou, and protect the home that has been in their family for many generations.

土楼家风家训

　　土楼人十分重视家风家训，每座土楼除了楼名以外，都有一副或者多副楹联，有的还将楼名巧妙地嵌入楹联里。楹联反映了土楼人家的世界观、人生观和价值观，彰显了良好的家风家训。楹联大多由当地名士撰写，并由书法名家和雕刻高手镌刻在土楼石门框或者厅堂里的柱子上，集诗、书、刻于一体的土楼楹联，形成教化、观赏、审美功能的景观，令人叹为观止。当然，也有一些楹联直接用油漆书写在木门框上，或者用墨水书写在红纸上张贴于大门两边。正是有了这些洋洋洒洒、各具特色、意义深远的土楼楹联，使得每一座土楼显得更有文化内涵，更有历史故事，更有诗情画意。

　　土楼民居的楹联内容或修身积德，或耕读兴家，或尊师重教，或忠孝报国，或宣扬家训，或赞美家园。字里行间无不传达着忠孝仁义礼智信、修身齐家治国平天下的哲理，表达出了土楼人家追求"真、善、美"的崇高品质，是教育家族后代的一种重要形式。

◎ 永定洪坑土楼群奎聚楼里的楹联。（王福平 摄）

Couplets in Kuijulou of Hongkeng Tulou Cluster in Yongding. (Photo by Wang Fuping)

◎ 永定洪坑土楼群振成楼里的楹联。（王福平 摄）

Couplets in Zhenchenglou of Hongkeng Tulou Cluster in Yongding. (Photo by Wang Fuping)

Family Precepts and Traditions in the Tulou

The Tulou residents place great importance upon family and discipline. Apart from the name of the Tulou that hangs at the front gate, each earthen building has one or more couplets. These couplets tend to subtly incorporate the name of the building and often reflect upon the world, life and the family values the Tulou residents uphold. Most of the couplets are written by famous locals and have been craved by calligraphy and engraving masters on the stone pillars either at the main Tulou gate or the hall. It is a breathtaking vision of poetry in the Tulou, creating a landscape of education, appreciation and aesthetics. Of course, some couplets have been directly painted on the wooden door frames, or written in ink on the red paper that is pasted on both sides of the door. It is these wordy perceptions that have been presented by unique words which make the Tulou the cultural, historical and poetic place that it is known to be.

Looking around the couplets in Tulou, there are many philosophical aspects and encouragements of loyalty, filial piety, righteousness, wisdom and self-cultivation of virtues. This represents the residents' pursuit of truth, goodness and beauty, which plays an important role in family education.

功名柱也是客家土楼人特有的家族传统教化文化。土楼人崇尚教育，鼓励子孙追求功名，家族里有人在科举考试中取得贡生以上的成绩时，就在家庙或家祠前为其立一根功名柱。每根功名柱背后都有一个成功族人的励志故事，既是对功名获得者的颂扬，也激励后人努力读书，光耀门庭。

Another traditional family culture unique to the Tulou Hakka residents is the special pillars that stand upright in front of the family temple. The Tulou people are strong advocates of education and descendants are always encouraged to pursue scholarly achievements. Back when imperial exams still existed, when someone scored a tribute or high rank a pillar of merit was set up. Behind every pillar is an inspirational story of success and acts as motivation for future generations to study hard.

◎ 南靖塔下村张氏家庙前的功名柱。（王福平 摄）
Pillars of merit in front of Zhang's family temple in Taxia Village, Nanjing. (Photo by Wang Fuping)

03
旅行规划

经典游一日线路

■ 永定土楼景区

线路一：**洪坑土楼群**（共7座世遗土楼，游览"土楼王子"振成楼、客家家训馆庆成楼、府第式土楼的杰出代表福裕楼、原生态的福兴楼、袖珍土楼如升楼、有婚庆民俗表演的光裕楼、颇具布达拉宫气势的奎聚楼，体验古老独特的夯墙技艺和木偶表演）——**高北土楼群**（共4座世遗土楼，游览"土楼王"承启楼、有方圆一线天独特景观的世泽楼、"不倒楼"五云楼、"博士楼"侨福楼）

线路二：**南溪土楼沟**（游览绵延十几千米的"土楼长城"，参观2座世遗土楼：被称作"土楼公主"的客家家风楼振福楼，外圆内方的衍香楼。夏季可体验"游人水中漂，土楼两岸走"的土楼第一漂，欣赏美丽的土楼夜景）——**初溪土楼群**（游览有10座世遗土楼的初溪古村落。"步步登高望景台，方圆楼顶似花开。溪边错落梯田绕，无限风光扑面来。"描绘的正是最令人震撼的初溪明清土楼群。古村占地面积仅15万平方米，却有36座大大小小、方圆各异的土楼分布其中）

■ 南靖土楼风景区

线路一：**田螺坑土楼群**（游览闻名世界的"四菜一汤"的5座世遗土楼）——**裕昌楼**（参观被称作"东倒西歪楼"也称"东歪西斜楼"的中华第一奇楼裕昌楼）——**河坑土楼群**（游览有着"仙山楼阁""北斗七星"之称的13座世遗土楼）

线路二：**田螺坑土楼群**（参观闻名世界的"四菜一汤"的5座世遗土楼）——**云水谣景区**（漫步历史悠久的古老村落，一边参观世遗土楼和贵楼及怀远楼，一边享受朴素恬静的乡野生活）

■ 华安大地土楼群

线路：**"土楼之王"二宜楼**（参观"之"字形传声洞、泄沙漏水孔、秘密地下通道、隐通廊、民间艺术珍品、西洋壁画等）——**南阳楼**（参观雕工精致的木雕石刻，体验天井中心的回音奇观）——**"最宜居的土楼"东阳楼**（感受土楼宜居舒适的环境，观赏方圆相济的土楼景观）——**民俗体验**（在土楼周边体验古老的制茶工艺，做麻糍、打贡糖等）

深度游主题线路

■ 永定客家文化体验之旅（一日）

客家博览园（探索悠久的客家历史文化，感悟客家深厚的文明真谛）——**福建土楼博物馆**（观看土楼与客家文化的展览，体会土楼与大自然的和谐共生）——**客家古镇**（感受历史穿越而来的客家古镇，体验独特的客家文化和特色小吃）

■ 永定土楼农耕观光之旅（一日）

陈东岩太高山土楼景区（被誉为"梯田上的家园""最具人间仙境景色之山村"）——**大溪坑头美丽乡村**（守艺人用最传统的方式制作器具、美食，传承着客家人的工匠精神）——**湖坑吴银梯田**（一片片梯田犹如横在天地间的一部厚重史诗，成为农耕文明的一道奇观）——**初溪土楼景区**（依山傍水，错落有致，体现出极高的美学艺术价值）

■ 南靖土楼古村之旅（二日）

南靖土楼二日游：抽出个小周末，花两天的时间在南靖土楼山水田园间游荡，感受山水田园相守的安然，远离喧嚣，心旷神怡。

田螺坑土楼群（游览闻名世界的"四菜一汤"田螺坑土楼群的5座世遗土楼）——**裕昌楼**（参观被称作"东倒西歪楼"的中华第一奇楼裕昌楼，品农家菜）——**塔下村**（漳州长寿第一村。有着近600年历史的古村落，处处小桥流水，各种形态的土楼沿溪而建，高低错落，在清澈的溪水中投射出别样的倒影，形成美妙的奇观）——**云水谣景区**（晚上宿云水谣，听溪流晚歌，观满天星辰）

云水谣景区（游览这个山川秀美、人文丰富的国家5A级景区，村中幽长古道、百年老榕、青砖古楼、小桥流水，无不令人流连忘返）——**和贵楼**（和贵楼是南靖已知的最高土楼，可以在天井里体验踩踩脚引起整片鹅卵石微微震动的感觉）——**怀远楼**（建筑工艺最精美、保护最好的双环圆形土楼）

■ 华安"探秘"之旅（一日）

沙建汰口古兵寨（探访古老兵寨的神秘）——**仙字潭**（领略上古仙人文字的神奇）——**新圩古渡口**（寻访古代闽西南水运码头）——**新圩官畲少数民族特色村寨**（体验畲家特有的民俗风情）——**大地土楼群**（参观世遗土楼二宜楼、南阳楼、东阳楼）

Tours Recommended

Classical Day-Trip Tours

■ Yongding Tulou Scenic Area

Option 1—1 Day

1) Hongkeng Tulou Cluster has a total of seven World Heritage buildings. Be sure to visit the following:

• Zhenchenglou – "the Prince of Tulou".

• Qingchenglou – The Hakka Family Precepts Centre.

• Fuyulou – a prime example of the ancient government complex architectural style.

• Fuxinglou – one of the most well preserved original Tulou.

• Rushenglou – the pocket Tulou.

• Guangyulou – the best place to observe wedding celebrations and folk performances.

• Kuijulou – having a similar architectural design to a palace, Kuijulou is the place to experience ancient puppet shows and witness the techniques used to create the building walls.

2) Gaobei Tulou Cluster has a total of four World Heritage buildings. Key areas to visit are:

• Chengqilou – known for its reputation as one of "the Kings of Tulou".

• Shizelou – this square Tulou has a unique view of the skyline.

• Wuyunlou – famous for its structure and is referred as "Never Falling Building".

• Qiaofulou – known for their scholars and academic achievements.

Option 2—1 Day

1) Nanxi Tulou Cluster, also known as "the Great Wall of Tulou", stretches over ten kilometres along a creek. A sight to behold, there are two main World Heritage Tulou to visit:

• Zhenfulou – known as "the Princess of Tulou" and brings alive the Hakka traditions.

• Yanxianglou – known for its peculiar shape of having a circular outer wall and square inner wall.

• In summer you can't miss rafting down the creek with rows of Tulou stretching along the bank.

2) Chuxi Tulou Cluster includes 10 World Heritage Tulou.

From the top of an observation deck, all the square and circular Tulou look like flowers. A stream winds its way around the terraced fields, creating a most stunning scene. The ancient village covers an area of 150,000 square metres yet, there spread 36 variously sized Tulou built in the Ming and Qing dynasties.

■ Nanjing Tulou Scenic Area

Option 3—1 Day

1) Tianluokeng Tulou Cluster:

This cluster has five famous Tulou – known as "the four dishes and one soup".

2) Yuchanglou:

Famous for its zigzag wooden post structure which has stood firm for centuries through natural elements and is often known as China's most mysterious building.

3) Hekeng Tulou Cluster:

Be sure to visit the 13 Tulou that are spread out in the shape of the big dipper constellation.

Option 4—1 Day

1) Tianluokeng Tulou Cluster:

This cluster has five famous Tulou – known as "the four dishes and one soup".

2) Yunshuiyao Scenic Area:

Walk through historic villages and explore Heguilou and Huaiyuanlou, also World Heritage listed buildings. This area provides a chance to immerse oneself in the rural life.

• Heguilou – the tallest Tulou in Nanjing. Come experience the vibrations through the cobblestone patio.

• Huaiyuanlou – the most beautiful and best protected concentric Tulou.

■ Huaǎn Dadi Tulou Cluster

Option 5—1 Day

Dadi Tulou Cluster is a great place to immerse yourself in ancient folk culture such as tea making techniques and making traditional sweets.

• Eryilou – known as another of "the Tulou kings". Notable features of this Tulou include a sound hole shaped like the Chinese character "之", its holes to filter out sand and water, secret underground passages, hidden corridors, folk art treasures and Western style murals.

• Nanyanglou – there are many carvings in wood and stone at this Tulou. In the centre of the courtyard, be sure to test out the echo resonance effect.

• Dongyanglou – Famed for being the most livable Tulou due to its comfortable environment and surrounding landscapes.

In-Depth Theme Tours

Option 1—1 Day

Yongding Hakka Cultural Experience Tour

- Hakka Expo Park – delve into the history of the Hakka civilisation.
- Fujian Tulou Museum – be sure to take a look around the exhibition to understand the Tulou and Hakka background. The museum is a great way to experience the harmonious symbiosis between the Tulou and nature.
- Hakka Ancient Town – walk through the streets and test special snacks and cultural activities that have been passed down through generations.

Option 2—1 Day

Yongding Tulou Agriculture Tour

- Yantai Tulou Scenic Area, Chendong – this area is known for the terraced fields and beautiful mountain scenery surrounding the Tulou village.
- Kengtou Village, Daxi – this place is renowned for its traditional artisan ways of making utensils, age-old craftsmanship and the cuisine of the Hakka people.
- Wuyin Terraces, Hukeng – the terraces are a depiction of a staircase that ties the heavens to the earth. It is an agricultural wonder.
- Chuxi Tulou Cluster – if you are drawn into aesthetics, then be sure to visit here to see the intertwining scenery of mountains and streams around the ancient Tulou village.

Option 3 —2 Days

Nanjing Tulou Ancient Village Tour

A perfect weekend tour, spend two days wandering the landscape surrounding Nanjing Tulou. Feel the tranquility of the mountains, water and fields in the countryside far away from the hustle and bustle of the city.

- Tianluokeng Tulou Cluster – this cluster has five famous Tulou – known as "the four dishes and one soup".
- Yuchanglou – famous for its zigzag wooden post structure which has stood firm for centuries through natural elements and is often known as China's most mysterious building.
- Taxia Village – with nearly 600 years of history, small bridges are scattered around the village between various forms of Tulou that have been built along the stream. The different sizes and shapes create a unique reflection upon the water's surface – a truly marvellous sight to behold. Stay in Yunshuiyao overnight and listen to the trickle of the stream while watching the stars in the night sky above.

- Yunshuiyao Scenic Area – visit the scenic spots that lie between mountains and rivers which have been given a 5A tourist rating. Here, you can find ancient roads that wind indefinitely through the village, ancient banyan trees and houses dotted here and there, and small bridges to help you get across the streams.
- Heguilou – the tallest Tulou in Nanjing. Come experience the vibrations through the cobblestone patio.
- Huaiyuanlou – the most beautiful and best protected concentric Tulou.

Option 4—1 Day

Tour of Hua'an's Mysteries

- Taikou Ancient War Village, Shajian – the mystery of the ancient fortress.
- Xianzitan – the magic of the ancient immortal script.
- Xinxu Ancient Ferry – go on a search for the ancient southwestern waterway terminal.
- Guanse Cultural Village of the Ethnic Minority She– experience the unique folk customs of the She people.
- Dadi Tulou Cluster – visit World Heritage buildings Eryilou, Nanyanglou and Dongyanglou.